Chapter1.

The Ford Anglia drew to a halt ___ ___-____ _____ looked at her husband, waiting for him to get out and open the door on her side; not that it was a gentlemanly thing that Charlie did for her but because it was jammed and could only be opened from the outside.

It seemed to take him ages to get to her side of the car but then he was suddenly there gesturing for her to lean on the door. As Charlie pulled on the door handle from the outside, she pushed as hard as she could from the inside until eventually, the door flew open and the bitter cold wind that blew straight off the River Mersey hit her and she shivered. Abigail knew that it wasn't just the cold, salty air making her shiver. The heater in the car had packed up and she was freezing. She was also terrified of being told that plans had changed and they would be leaving empty handed, and this was adding to the shivers. Well, that's what she said it was but in reality, Abigail knew she was shaking with fear.

She didn't think she could cope if she had to hear the dreadful noises that she had heard the first time. It took her months to stop having nightmares and she didn't want to have to go through that again. The first time, even though the noise really disturbed her, it was just small and manageable but this one, the third attempt was bigger and definitely established.
She had been warned that it wouldn't be easy but was determined to see it through. "Please God, let it work," she murmured.

She didn't think she could bear it again, being told that plans had changed so suddenly like they had the second time. All that travelling for nothing. It was such a long way to York and for what? All her plans for the future in tatters and leaving with nothing but broken dreams and the desperate need to feel whole snatched from her at the last minute. She knew that if it didn't happen this time, then there were no more chances. They had agreed, her and Charlie, that she would just have to be satisfied with what they had.

Abigail clambered out of the car and stared intently at each window of the impressive building that stood in its own grounds, trying to catch a glimpse of the women who were housed here and wondering if she would get to meet the one woman who would change everything for so many people.

She breathed in deeply as she walked towards the gate and as she did so, she noticed that this house had a name rather than a number. Berkeley House was perfectly chiselled into the large gate posts, one word on each, and once Abigail had gone through the gate, up the
winding path and into the building, she silently prayed that her dreams would hopefully become a reality.

They had come all the way from Burscough to this place called Blundellsands and now they were here, Abigail wanted the reason for their journey over and done with as smoothly and quickly as possible. This was the worst bit, but soon she could put the events that were to unfold behind her and it would not have to be mentioned again, that she had ever had to make this journey to such a place. Life would be different for all of them involved in a couple of hours and the less fuss that was made, the better. No matter how it worked out.

Charlie opened the gate and ushered his wife through. He knew that she was worried even though she hadn't said a word. The look on her face said it all. He wasn't a religious man but as he looked at Abigail's eyes that were brimming with tears, he patted her arm and said, "Come on love, it will be all right this time, God only knows how on earth this one could go wrong. We know that the woman has agreed and is chomping at the bit to get back to her family in Lancashire. If there is such a thing as God, I am sure he will make it work this time".

He grinned at her cheekily, passed her a cloth handkerchief and waited for her to wipe her eyes, then, holding her arm, he led her to the front door and rang the bell.

Chapter 2.

They stood, each wrapped up in their own thoughts and as they heard the sudden, loud grating sound of a key turning, they both jumped. Abigail's legs turned to jelly and she grabbed her husband's arm to steady herself. Then the door opened. A woman in a nurse's uniform that was covered with an exceptionally clean apron ushered them into the entrance hall, and once the married couple were inside, quietly closed the door and locked it. That grating sound of the door being locked brought a feeling of fear to Abigail and she suddenly felt as though she was imprisoned.

This was eerie, thought Abigail as she looked around her. It didn't look right. The entrance hall was too clean, almost sterile, and the highly polished bannister of the staircase reminded her of a stately home. Then, as she looked down a dismal corridor, she realised that this building was completely silent. There was no noise and that was a worry. A place like this should have noise, not this oppressive silence. This building, thought Abigail, held such sadness and she was sure she could feel it rising from the highly polished floor that she was rooted to. An involuntary tremor ran through her as she heard the nurse speak in a broad Liverpudlian accent that was far too friendly under the circumstances. Abigail instinctively knew that the woman's tone was just for show and took an instant dislike to this nurse in a starched apron. Even though the nurse was smiling, it didn't take that cold look from her eyes.

"Good afternoon, I am Sister Kelp and I presume that you are Mr and Mrs Hennessey? It's a pleasure to meet you. Did you have a good journey? I hope you found us easily? Matron is waiting to speak with you before… well… you know? I'll go in the office and tell her you are here. Won't be a 'mo'".

As this contradiction of a woman spoke, her voice echoed around the hallway and seemed to float up the stairs before dying away. Then the nurse quickly turned and went into a room leaving heavy footsteps to echo emptily before firmly shutting the door behind her.

Abigail nudged Charlie, whispering so that her voice would not resonate around the emptiness and making sure she wouldn't be heard.

"This place is horrible Charlie. What on earth have we come to? You can't hear any noise and there should be noise. I really don't like it and that nurse is…"

Abigail stopped whispering as the door opened and Sister Kelp invited them to step inside the office. Then the nurse quietly closed the door and left them to speak with the Matron.

Once inside, the first thing Abigail saw was an enormous dark wooden desk that had a large gleaming brass plaque with the word "Matron" inscribed. Abigail felt uncomfortable as the small woman stood up and asked them to sit on chairs placed strategically on the far wall near the door they had just come through. It was as though this woman wanted them as far away from her position of power as possible. As they walked towards the chairs, Charlie lifted his, motioned for his wife to do the same and they both placed them closer to the desk then sat down.

"I think it is better if we are closer to you, then we will not mishear anything you have to tell us," Charlie calmly stated. His eyes locked with Matron's as he spoke and his tone made it perfectly clear to her that he was not a man to be disregarded or messed with.

Matron cleared her throat nervously, nodded and smiled thinly.

"As you like Mr Hennessey," she said, "but please be aware that if there is any upset and you have to leave quickly, you are now putting yourself, your wife and the reason for your visit at a disadvantage and that is something I always try to avoid. It's better for everyone if the disposal process that we run here is kept to. If things get out of hand, we have, on occasion, had to call for the police for help in restraining certain ones who think they can beat the system. Not something I want here.

Charlie sat bolt upright on his seat, then, leaning towards the desk began to speak quietly.

"May I inform you, Matron," he said, "that I am the police and however you run your so called "process" for this very emotional and difficult event, to me sounds as though you have not one care for anyone else but yourself. If, as you say, there could be upset, then we will deal with that should the need arise. Are you not aware that you are dealing with people who will have to live with the consequences of their actions or actions that have been forced on them forever? Surely this place that is linked to such a wonderful religion and here to help others should be run in a more compassionate manner? I dread to think of the treatment that is meted out in here if the very person who is supposedly in charge and employed to support has so little respect for those concerned. We are talking of lives of real people here, not animal carcasses to be despatched from a bloody slaughterhouse! Now, are you ready to begin with the formalities? I think that the sooner my wife and I are out of your company and leave here, the better."

Matron lowered her eyes and reached over for a file at the corner of the desk. Her hands were shaking, not from the shock of being spoken to in such a manner, although that had definitely unsettled her, but they shook due to the fact that she desperately needed a quick vodka to get her senses on a more even keel in case she had to face any further aggravation from this man. She was wondering if he was highly ranked in the police force, highly enough to make waves once they had gone.

What if he sent someone to the hostel to talk with the women?

Would these women be believed?

Would that dreadful woman, Sister Kelp, be loyal to her and take her side?

All this because of two chairs. Anyway, one thing she was sure about was that she wanted these two out of here as soon as possible. Mr Hennessey was not someone to be messed with and she didn't like feeling scared. He had no right to speak to her like that.

The Church was happy with the way she ran things; in fact she was encouraged to be harsh. A mortal sin had to be dealt with fully and effectively so that these creatures would understand the error of their ways and that God may, one day, forgive them. Her treatment of these disgusting, unholy beings fitted the sin. She was doing a good job.

Yes, she thought. These people should be grateful to her. If the hostel wasn't here, then this couple would not become parents to one of the long line of bastards that she had to put up with until they were either shipped out to a family that was meant to fit the real mother in some way or dumped in an orphanage until they were adults. Either way, it was no real
concern of hers what happened to these brats. The best thing about them going was that a new fallen woman would take their place and that meant her job was safe.

Mr Hennessey could go to Hell in a handcart as far as she was concerned and take his wife and new daughter with him once he had signed some paperwork. Now, where was that damned social worker? Nothing could be done or signed until it was witnessed. Matron rang a bell that was on the desk shaking it to make the most noise possible.

****

The door opened almost instantly and Sister Kelp stood looking smugly at the Matron.

"Did you want me or do you want me to fetch the social worker? I put her in the kitchen until you were ready as you seemed a bit, well, involved in a conversation that was obviously private to the hostel only".

The Sister's eyes glinted with a look that implied she had heard everything and that she had taken great enjoyment from hearing someone put this small drunkard of a woman in her place.

The nurse really hoped that this copper would report her boss as it was about time that she was brought down a peg or two. She was sick of being treated like muck and given all the rubbish jobs to deal with. If Matron was reported and if it meant she lost her job, then so be it. There was no way she would take the side of the woman whom she loathed but had to call Matron; a Matron who delighted in being cruel just because she could.

But really, the last thing Sister Kelp wanted to do was to leave Berkeley House. The money was better in any of the many factories that Liverpool boasted than what she got paid here and at least she would go home cleaner and not covered in all kinds of vile fluids and foul smells if she lost her job. Her own sister and mother kept on at her to leave but if truth be known, she would only jump when she had to. They only wanted her to leave because of what the hostel represented and, in their minds, no good Catholic woman should be mixing with this type of person.

What if the job carried a stigma with it that made people either ignore you or want to know so much about the hostel that she had to be blunt when refusing to talk? You could never be too careful as you might be talking to a relative, an undercover investigator from the Church or even worse, the press.

It was the babies that kept her working here in more ways than one and she was shrewd enough to know that there would be babies here for many years to come. They would all be hidden in plain sight, just like the little moneymaking scheme that the babies had helped her develop. This job had its perks and there were not many places where you could get food cooked for you every day and eat as much as you wanted and was totally free. It was easy to fiddle a bit of cash from the Giro run and the best of all, have constant access to milk powder, creams and nappies that fetched a pretty penny when she sold them on. She could make nearly as much from her perks as she got paid each month and would be a fool to let go of something so easy to fiddle, difficult to prove and she was well fed into the bargain. Fresh meat twice a week was a luxury, and tasted all the better for being free.

Sister Kelp knew she was on a good thing here and even if the copper did kick up a fuss, it would soon be silenced as nobody wanted to acknowledge a place like this existed in the posh part of Liverpool. As far as she was concerned, out of muck came money and these filthy women who were worse than muck in her eyes, were nothing more than cash cows.

****

The social worker stood next to the desk looking through the file for the relevant papers. When she had found what she was looking for, she turned to face the couple who were sitting stony faced. She was aware that the man was really angry. She wondered what had happened in here and instinctively knew that the Matron would be at the back of it. This wasn't the first time she had met prospective parents in this office who were either very uncomfortable, upset or angry and the Matron had always been the instigator with her snide comments and total disregard for the need for decorum.

She had to admit to herself that this situation and the meeting to sign papers was always difficult and emotionally charged but she instinctively knew that this meeting had not gone well, in fact from the atmosphere, really badly would be a better way to describe it. No doubt she would find out what had happened the next time she was here. All she wanted to do now, was get the baby away and get the woman who had brought the child into the world to Lime Street station where her family were waiting to meet her.

"Mr and Mrs Hennessey, it's good to see you again," she said. "Just a few loose ends to tidy up and then we can go and fetch the baby. Oh, no we aren't doing that with this one. I gave my word to the woman who is giving up the baby that she can hand her over to you yourself, Mrs Hennessey. Will that be all right? I can guarantee that there will be no fuss, as
the woman is desperate to go and get on with her life. She has given me her word that she will be sensible. She wants to do it the right way and she wants to meet you. I know that might be something of a shock, but I think it will help both of you, especially you, Mrs Hennessey, after the first time".

Abigail looked at her husband and then at the Matron.

"I will meet her and if it makes it easier for the baby to be given to us, then that can only be a good thing. You never know, I might even get on with her, the mother that is. I don't suppose she will have had too much kindness shown to her in here. It's her final request and I would be honoured to make sure that it happens. After all, I will be the baby's mum soon and I want this lady to know that the baby will be well cared for and loved."

As the Matron let out a snort of derision, Abigail stood and asked where she needed to sign. She stared intently at the Matron until the Matron looked away. Then she turned to her husband, smiled and told him that he would be better to stay where he was and complete the paperwork. Glaring once more at the Matron, Abigail turned and followed the social worker to where she was to meet her daughter's first mother who would, in a very short time have nothing more than a few months' worth of memories to remember this child's life by.

A new way of living for all concerned was only moments away.

The two women looked at each other. Abigail was astonished to see that the woman in front of her was not a young mother but she looked to be in her late twenties or early thirties.

The social worker introduced the two by first names only. She said that she would give them five minutes to chat and then it would be time to head to the train station. She made quite
sure that both women were sitting on the battered settee before she left the room, telling them that she was just in the hallway should they want her.

Abigail nodded and moved closer to the woman to get a glimpse of the sleeping baby girl that was soon to be her daughter. The woman had instinctively pulled the baby closer to her when Abigail moved and this made the child squirm but not waken.

"We will keep her middle name as Theresa as you wanted and she will be raised as a Catholic until she is old enough to have her own opinions and choices," Abigail said, her eyes not moving from the baby's face. "She has an older brother and I am sure he will be thrilled with her when they meet. We will do the best we can to give her a good life and we will keep her safe. I know it will take time for the little one to settle but in time, all will be well."

It was at this point that Lizzie Brady stood and offered her daughter to this woman called Abigail, a woman who Lizzie was now trusting the daughter she could not keep to be her new mother. As Abigail stood, her arms came forward and she took the baby. Lizzie said, "Yes, all will be well," and left the room quickly leaving her daughter to start a new life with her new mother.

Abigail stared at the door that Lizzie had just gone out of and felt really quite sad for the woman. She was amazed at the composure that the woman had shown and the speed with which she had relinquished the baby. It was almost as though the woman called Lizzie was relieved it was over. It was as though the woman had not one bit of emotion in her body for this child. Abigail could not fathom out how someone could be so detached about giving up a baby.

She had expected tears from the birth mother, well some sort of scene to be honest, as this was what had happened when they collected the first baby that they had adopted. That birth mother had been hysterical and the sounds that had emanated from that small young woman were something Abigail hoped to never hear again. It was the sound of raw grief, painful, harrowing and very disturbing. The screams of that woman had haunted Abigail for months after she and Charlie had run down the corridor in the convent in Surrey, nuns behind them
holding the poor woman back and nuns either side of them urging them to hurry. She had been bundled into the car, the baby almost thrown onto her knee and Charlie was told to go as fast as he could until they were out of sight. As the car

sped off, Abigail thought she saw someone fighting with the nuns, but convinced herself that she was wrong. It was too much to bear, knowing that this boy, who was now her son, had had a mother who was under the impression she could keep her child and had had him ripped from her arms minutes after they had signed that form. That poor young girl had been well and truly lied to.

Abigail could not believe how smoothly it had gone for her this time and turned her attention to the sleeping child. She stared at the tiny face taking in every detail; the closed eyes with long brown lashes, the shape of soft feathery eyebrows, the chubby cheeks, the button nose and the little mouth, slightly open as the tiny thumb had fallen when that deep relaxing sleep had enveloped the child completely. Her little hand made a fist with the thumb, damp with saliva, lying still by her face.

Only when the door opened and her husband came to her side did she take her eyes off the child. In a low voice that was choking with emotion Abigail kept repeating over and over again, "She is ours", until blinded by tears of joy, she passed the baby to her new father. This one will be different, Abigail thought, as she reached for her handkerchief and wiped away
the tears. As she stood watching her husband hold their new daughter, she felt as though her life were complete. She was married to a man of status. A mother of two children. One boy, one girl. The perfect family. It was a family who she knew had been engineered from other people's misfortunes, but that unfortunate start in life could now be disregarded by her and would never be fully revealed to the children. That was the law. Once the judge had granted them legal ownership of a child and the adoption was complete, the children's past would disappear, never to be raised or spoken of again unless it was absolutely necessary.

The social worker gave them some baby milk, half a dozen terry towelling nappies and some waterproof pants to see them over until they got organised and said she would be round to see them next week. The time of the appointment was on the card in the bag.

"It's time to leave now. I am sure that your little boy will be missing you and wondering where you are", the social worker said as she looked with delight at the scene in front of her.

She liked her job. It was a mixture of sadness and joy but it was always about the babies for her. Seeing them placed with people who had been vetted so that there was no doubt they would be good parents and that the child would be raised properly, always gave her a sense of achievement. She thought of herself as a quiet life changer who could be proud of all those
children that she organised proper families for and she loved the thanks that was lavished on her on days like this. Now all she had to do was get rid of them and take Lizzie Brady to Lime Street and she could go home and get ready to go dancing.

"Let me get the door for you while you wrap the baby up in her shawl properly. It's still a bitter wind out there and the last thing we want her to take with her is a bad cold. Now, if you are ready, let's get you going. The sooner you get back home, the sooner you can all get to know each other", the social worker said encouragingly.

Once again, the key turned in the lock and that dreadful grating sound was heard but this time not as loudly. It was muted by the sound of babies crying, a crescendo of noise that echoed up the staircase and faded slowly. Abigail shivered uncontrollably as she heard the wails of so many more babies and wondered if they would be found happy families and be saved from the shame of their beginnings. It was almost as if those babies were saying goodbye to her daughter and for some reason, it unsettled her.

Mr and Mrs Hennessey walked down the path towards the car. Eventually, they got the passenger door open and before Abigail got in, she turned and looked at the grand house, staring at every window, hoping never to see this place that was so full of sadness again, for
as long as she lived. Then with a sigh, she clambered onto the front seat, pulled the door firmly shut and took the baby from her husband. Once she was settled, the car pulled away taking her and her daughter on a new road and to a new way of life.

Chapter 3.

Hannah Theresa Hennessey did nothing but cry. Abigail was totally at a loss as to why her daughter just would not stop crying. It was getting on her nerves as it had been going on for weeks.

If she looked at Hannah, or sat her daughter on her knee, tried to play little games with her or rocked her in the big carriage-built pram this child still cried. Great big tears flowed down her chubby cheeks, sobs were accompanied by rivers of snot and saliva that messed up her daughter's pretty clothes and made Hannah sticky and even more distressed when Abigail tried desperately to clean her face. When she tried to cuddle Hannah and sing soothing songs, Abigail noticed that her daughter went rigid in her arms, sometimes to the point that the baby was difficult to handle and had to be put down quickly so that Hannah might relax and Abigail wouldn't drop her.

They had been to the doctor with Hannah to see if she was poorly but had been told that she was as healthy as any seven-month-old baby was likely to be. The only time she was not crying was when she was eating or drinking her bottle of milk before bedtime. But even that suppertime bottle was a challenge. Why Hannah refused her bottle if she was held in
Abigail's arms was a mystery. Even Charlie had no chance of feeding her and he had loads of experience with babies. They had found that the best way to get her to drink was by laying her on the couch and propping the bottle up. They sat next to her and were aware that Hannah's eyes never left their body, but if they looked directly at her or spoke to her, then all hell broke loose and the crying started along with the choking and gagging as she inhaled milk with each long breath but which was thankfully followed by that ear splitting scream as she

breathed out between tiny front teeth that were clamped onto the teat.

The sobs and screams got louder as the bottle was taken forcefully out of the little one's mouth so that she didn't cause real damage to herself, but there was no way that Hannah would drink any more milk if this happened, even if she had actually calmed down enough to be offered it again. All this waste was costing money, Abigail commented to her daughter as once again she was met with refusal and watched helplessly as her daughter twisted her head frantically every time the bottle came towards her mouth.

Another thing Abigail noticed was that Hannah rarely smiled but would stare intently at her and Charlie. Surely by now, she should have got used to their faces and be able to recognise them as her mummy and daddy? The only person that this child was comfortable with was her brother John, and Hannah would gurgle, smile and laugh for him.

This was really upsetting for Abigail as her son, John, was never like this. In fact, when he was adopted, he was so quiet that she and Charlie never knew what it was to have to make him to calm. He only grizzled now and then and was happy to be held and had always to be close to her, his mother. His big brown eyes followed her everywhere but he never really cried, not like Hannah. In fact, he rarely made any noise or spoke much either even though he was four years old now.

She had tried to talk to Charlie about Hannah's incessant crying through the day but he said it was for her to deal with. Didn't he do his fair share at night when he was pacing the floors until the crack of dawn? He couldn't do it all and work as well but he did do his share, especially when Abigail was so exhausted that she literally couldn't stop herself from screaming at the baby to stop and held her down onto the mattress, forcing her to be still and begging her to lie down and go to sleep.

Abigail had desperately written to her own mother for advice but was told that if the child was not ill, was thriving and growing then there was nothing to worry about. Even the weekly visit from the social worker didn't help, as Hannah would be more than happy to smile at her and reach for a cuddle whenever she appeared. Abigail had to pretend that Hannah was as good as gold when that woman came around as the last thing that she wanted to happen was for her to let slip that she was struggling to cope with the baby and the constant crying. The social worker might stop the adoption and Abigail was terrified of that happening. They were still being monitored as acceptable parents for Hannah and the baby could be taken away on a whim, if the social worker so desired.

It wasn't as though there was no routine for Hannah; it was almost as though she refused to follow the routine. It might help, thought Abigail, if her daughter would somehow learn to sleep through the night. The notes from the hostel said that she was sleeping right through and only woke for a few minutes on occasion but was easily soothed and went back to sleep. The notes also said that Hannah was a happy baby who smiled a lot. Well, as far as Abigail was concerned, this child certainly did not match the notes in any way shape or form and wondered if she had been given another baby's copy because of all the carry on with that horrible Matron from that hostel.

"Please Charlie, will you at least consider asking if you can have just one more week on earlies"? Abigail cajoled as she slipped her arm around her husband's broad back and rested her hand on his stomach, taking comfort from his muscled form and feeling safe, secure and brave enough to voice her concerns again, as she lay in bed.

A broken record was what Charlie called her, and yes, she did feel like the needle was stuck on that single record and played the same few words and part of the strained melody over and over. It was the strained melody of her own inadequacy as a mother to her daughter, whilst Hannah cried, words that were misunderstood as being difficult and stubborn and her inability as a baby to move to the next part of the song that was unfamiliar, her new, alien world.

"She's doing much better at sleeping longer and thankfully not crying as much through the day but I don't think I am ready to manage her on my own if she wakes in the night and won't settle for me," Abigail added as she gently moved her hand to caress his chest.

Charlie sighed and turned over onto his back, placing his arms above his head. As he stared at nothing in particular on the ceiling, he took a moment before he answered.

"Abigail, we've been over this time and again. You are doing a great job with Hannah and the more she gets used to you dealing with her, the quicker she's going to adjust. I've told you what to do. Make sure that she has that shawl to hand, you know, the one she came with, when you put her in the cot. She's really attached to it and you can see how tightly she holds onto it. Just make sure that she doesn't hear your voice if you have to go in and sort her
out. Babies are cleverer than we give them credit for. They can pick up on so much and if we are upset, then so are they. It's the only way she can tell us that she's not happy at the moment but as she gets bigger and we can get her round to our way of thinking, all this will become just a distant memory. Trust me, I know what I'm talking about. I was the oldest of six, remember, and had to just about bring up the two youngest for my mum.   I'll tell you what we will do. We'll go out for an hour or two tomorrow with the kids, take them for a walk by the old airfield and to the park. If they

get loads of fresh air and we keep Hannah from falling asleep if she gets tired while we are out, then I'm sure she will sleep better tomorrow night for you. It will do John good too, to have a run around and explore those old huts used as billets. You never know, it might liven him up a bit, bring him out of his shell and get him talking a bit more if he sees and does something new. I know you can do this Abigail so stop worrying over nothing. You are meeting all her needs and there is absolutely nothing wrong with Hannah. The social worker says you are a brilliant mum. Now, come here and give your old man a kiss and a cuddle whilst the little wilful wailer of a wildcat, who will soon be our daughter for keeps, is asleep."

As Charlie turned to face his wife and sought her lips in the darkened room, that all too familiar wail sailed in through slightly open bedroom door. Bloody hell, thought Charlie as he kissed his wife, let the brat wait. My needs have to be met too.

It was his fourth shift on nights, the last one and then he had three days of rest before he went back onto earlies. Abigail was getting the children ready for bed. The bath was running and as she carried Hannah from the bedroom, she shouted for Charlie to bring John upstairs.

Bath time was a rarity for the children and if truth be told, for Abigail too and she was looking forward to getting into the lukewarm, used water once the children were clean and wrapped in towels. Charlie had agreed to dry and dress the two of them and settle them down for her so she could hopefully have at least twenty minutes soaking her cares away as long as there was some warmth in the water and obviously, Hannah behaved and didn't start to cry. She knew Charlie would demand that Abigail came to sort out the baby immediately and she would have to do as he said. Charlie had to start getting ready for work and any delay in his routine would be unthinkable. As he had told her, he could spare her half an hour. It was quite a novelty that her husband had said yes to helping her and although she was grateful, knew it was only because she had to get the children out early in the morning so that he could catch up on his sleep and have peace and quiet to do so once they had gone. He never did anything for no return that would benefit him. There was always a condition attached.

Abigail was taking the children to Preston for the day to look around the market. She was looking forward to the change of scenery and being with people of her own kind. People who
spoke like her and had the same outlook on life that she was missing since moving to Burscough and had to pretend she was someone that she wasn't and didn't want to be. She didn't know how to learn to be what her husband wanted her to be and was always scared to let him down.

The children had to pass his approval before they left the house tomorrow, as did she, and they had to stand there and be inspected for cleanliness and tidiness before he let them out. Only then would he give her some money for the train fare and a little bit more for a bite of food and a drink for her and John. Hannah had to make do with a jar of cold baby food and a bottle of milk.

As she stood by the bath, Abigail's mind wandered. She was convinced that her daughter had something wrong in her that made it impossible for her to stop crying once she had started, but had to admit that the little one was getting better and had actually slept the whole night after their day out in the fresh air. Abigail smiled to herself as she thought about the feeling of panic that rose in her when she had woken before her daughter and had dashed into the room and peered anxiously into the cot, hoping that Hannah was just asleep and nothing more. Was that a sign that she had accepted her daughter, warts and all? Abigail knew no two babies were the

same, but Hannah was such a handful, she had actually thought for one
fleeting moment of handing her back before the adoption was finalised but knew it was only because she had been exhausted.

Abigail wished that she could have a bath all to herself more often as she tested the heat of the water and lowered Hannah into the clean tub. It would soon be filled with a grey scum from the soap, but it used up too much money to heat the water for everyone. It meant two extra shovels of coal on the fire, which was a luxury they could ill afford now they had another mouth to feed. Charlie had to have a bath every day but it didn't use any extra coal to heat the water for just one decent bath and she could manage quite well with a pan of hot water from the stove if she needed an extra wash at night and was quick enough to get every bit of her body done before it went cold.

Charlie's position in life dictated that he had to be exceptionally well turned out, even on his days off. He had to keep up appearances he said. It was what people who had middle class professions had to do. His status in life as a policeman had to be maintained in a way that was fitting and so that people knew he had to be respected. Charlie was proud of his rise in society and often told her that she had to leave behind her working-class background and get used to being a middle-class housewife and mother, befitting of his expectations. That
was why he scrutinised her and the children before they went out anywhere, especially if they had to walk near the police station.

Sunday night was bath night, and the rest of the time it was a strip wash in the kitchen for her and John with one dish of water between them every morning. As long as hands, face, feet and private bits were washed daily, then they could manage to stay clean. Hannah was dumped in the old Belfast sink every night as she was still small enough to fit and until she was out of nappies this ensured she was properly clean and didn't get a sore bottom.

This bath night was special as it meant that tomorrow, they could get breakfast together when Charlie was back from work, the children dressed after a quick wipe with the flannel and then they would be on their way, after inspection, of course. Abigail felt happier than she had done for a few weeks and began to sing to her daughter who was chewing on a little yellow duck. Hannah looked at her mother and smiled. A real smile that warmed Abigail's heart and helped to melt away a tiny bit of the stress that she was hiding. When Abigail sang louder, Hannah laughed and offered her mother the duck. "Mama, Mama," she chortled as Abigail took the offering and wriggled it in the air. Hannah splashed delightedly, and as Abigail reached for the towel to dry her face from her daughter's game, she was able to hide the fact that she was crying tears of joy that this child had, at long last, acknowledged her as her mother.

****

The children were asleep. Hannah had been so good thought Abigail as she rested her knitting on her knee and rubbed her tired eyes. Her daughter had fallen asleep almost as soon as she was laid down and given that shawl that she loved so much. Hopefully Hannah would sleep through tonight and then Abigail would be fresh for the outing tomorrow and not get too tired or irritable and they could all have a wonderful time. John, as usual, just got on with it. Her son knew he had to do as he was told, especially when Charlie was around and was totally compliant with whatever was expected of him. Abigail was delighted with her son. He was always such a good, quiet little boy who was no trouble. In fact, she hardly knew she had him, as most of the time he was happy in his own company playing with his toy cars. She loved to listen to him pretending to drive the cars and talking to himself, ordering people around and demanding that they did things now, or else there would be trouble and he would hit them. It was uncanny how he spoke exactly like Charlie did, even though they were rarely together. She wondered where it came from, her adopted son's attitude. Probably from his birth mother, she thought. Yes! He had inherited her attitude for being quiet but aggressive if the need arose. Well, wasn't she fighting with the holy sisters when they took John away? Abigail returned to her knitting, satisfied that her explanation of her son's aggressive play was nothing to do with her or Charlie.

Charlie was polishing his boots in the kitchen and she felt a certain pride as she heard the occasional sound of him spit lightly onto the leather before he continued to work in the shoe polish to make the toecaps gleam. So many people commented on his boots and shoes and how Charlie always looked so smart no matter when they saw him. It was a credit to her, they said, how well she looked after her husband. His clothes were always immaculately laundered and pressed to perfection and Abigail gladly accepted this praise and recognition from acquaintances, as it was very rare it came from her husband. In fact, he was sometimes too quick to make her feel inadequate even though he had taught her how to iron his clothes, as he said, properly.

Spit and polish Charlie called it. A throw back to his army days, well, National Service that was mandatory for all men who were white British and aged 17 or above and were fit and healthy. Charlie had served two years and then he had enlisted for a further four years. He would have stayed in the Army but there had been a bit of bother just as he came to the end of his time. He hadn't been court-martialled, but had been demoted back to the rank of

Private and that meant a drop down in pay. Charlie was so aggrieved, he felt that he had to leave rather than sign on again.

He liked the routine in the army and found that the uniform made him feel important and gave him a sense of pride, of being different, having respect given because of what he wore. A cut above was what Charlie had to be.

Back in Civvy Street, his long-term prospects were hardly what he classed as having that something different, something that would make him feel better about his poor upbringing in the grimy cobbled streets of Accrington. It wasn't just that he was brought up in a place where working classes were expected to do mundane jobs in factories or mills from the age of fifteen and have no desire to do anything else, it was due to the fact that he was the oldest of six children and had experienced nothing but raw poverty for as long as he could remember. The lack of food, warmth and love that his mother felt was not a priority had lit a fire in his belly that was the driving force to have much better as an adult and escape his terrible childhood. He wanted something that meant he could rise through the ranks of both social standing and earning power. That something was the police force and Abigail knew how much it meant for him to have this better way of life, a good wage that was a reflection of his
success and now have the added kudos of a family, who to strangers in the outside world were theirs by blood.

She would try harder to be how he needed her to be, she thought, as the knitting needles clicked together and another stitch was formed. After all, if she could convince him she was what he expected her to be, it would make her life a whole lot easier and maybe one day he would be able to completely forgive her for not being able to give him real children of his own. He had only agreed to the adoption of children so that it would not be considered that he was not a real man who could not sire children. He had said as much after the tests proved it was her that would be barren and never experience the joy of childbirth. Even though he had later apologised to Abigail, she knew Charlie had meant it and it had hurt her very much.

She sensed that deep down, this would eventually drive a wedge between them and he would abandon her. Charlie's mother had warned her that he would one day turn and walk away to someone who was normal in that department and she was on borrowed time. Charlie's life had to be perfect, or rather, his idea of perfect. Abigail would prove her witch of a mother-in -law wrong, starting from now. She would keep her husband and live as a married woman with a family no matter what it took.

Charlie stormed into the parlour waving a shirt wildly, his eyes cold and his lips drawn into a tight line that was holding back the cutting words he was working up to say. Abigail looked up at the shirt and then, quickly averting her eyes, placed the knitting that she was still working on, onto the floor.

"Look at this", Charlie hissed as he threw the shirt at his wife. "If you expect me to wear this, you can think again. That collar is a damned disgrace".

Abigail looked at the offending part of the shirt and sighed.

"It's a tiny mark and it will be hidden by your tunic, Charlie. I did tell you that I couldn't get it all out. I scrubbed it to the point I thought that the collar would fray. There's that new pack of collars upstairs and I'm sure it will be all right for you to use one of those just for tonight. I'll go and get one for you now and run the iron over it".

As she stood, Charlie shook his head, a look of disdain covered his face and he glared at her as she passed him and left the room. Abigail knew she was in trouble as she quietly made her way upstairs. It was a shirt collar for goodness sake and she now had to placate her husband somehow and make sure he went to work feeling happy. Hopefully, the new collar wouldn't rub his neck during the night as it would be the silent treatment for her in the morning. When the children were present Charlie never argued or shouted too much at her in front of them.

She debated waking Hannah up. If the girl was awake Abigail knew that the crying would start and she would get away with not being made to feel worthless and stupid and with a bit of luck, she would be able to keep out of Charlie's way until he went to work. After all, her daughter's needs came first. But what if Hannah wouldn't settle? No. Abigail would just take what was to come. Hannah had to stay asleep. Charlie had to leave for work in fifteen minutes so it wouldn't be that bad as he didn't have time for a full-blown showdown.

Charlie ranted on and on as he struggled to fix the stiff unwashed piece of material onto his shirt. The stud hole on the collar was rigid and he was getting more and more irate with each attempt to push the little brass circle into place. Abigail offered to help, her voice soft and sympathetic in an attempt to calm Charlie but it had completely the opposite effect.

Charlie started speaking through gritted teeth.

"Keep out of my way. A bloody useless woman is what you are. This is all your fault. How you can't wash a collar properly is beyond me but to try to hide the fact that you are so thick and can't do the simplest of jobs shows how useless you are. I have *told* you how to wash them. I have *shown* you how to wash them, but no, still too hard for you to get right Abigail. Do I have to do everything? You had better make sure those children are spotless tomorrow or you won't be going anywhere. Do I make myself clear?"

Charlie's voice got louder and louder until Abigail felt sure that the neighbours would be able to hear through the walls. She nodded, knowing that to speak before he told her to would continue to inflame the situation and then the neighbours would definitely hear and be asking questions that she didn't dare answer, even though they were genuinely concerned for her. When his voice thundered around the parlour shouting, "Answer me woman, did you not hear me?" she stood as straight as she could and mustered every ounce of courage.

"I heard you Charlie," she replied. "I think half the street has heard you tonight. But don't you worry about that. I will just make it all right for you, like any good wife would. Now, if you don't get a move on, you'll be late for work. Oh, and yes, you have made yourself perfectly clear".

Shaking, Abigail sat down, picked up her knitting and the pattern and began to look for the next set of instructions. As the back door slammed shut, the pattern became blurry as her tears made the ink run down the cheap paper. She cried silently, waiting for that all too familiar sound that heralded the fact that her daughter was well and truly awake. The noise Charlie had made was enough to waken the dead and so she listened for the wail.

****

Hannah was hysterical. Her tiny chest heaved as her breathing increased with each cry and she battled to refill her lungs, getting ready for the next volley of sobs and screams. The frightened baby clung to the collar of Abigail's cardigan with one hand and would not let go. The other hand waved wildly and the arm had developed a life of its own as it flailed around indiscriminately, catching Abigail full in the face and then rebounding into the open space. Hannah's chubby legs were like pistons on a steam engine moving backwards and forwards, giving the impression that she was running, desperate to get away from this situation. Abigail was at her wit's end. This had been going on for an hour and a half now. Every time she had managed to sooth her daughter to the point that she wasn't crying and tried to lie her in the cot, Hannah once again began kicking and screaming until there was no other choice but to lift her up and start again, trying to calm her down.

Her head was thumping and Abigail was hoping that she wasn't heading for a full-blown migraine. That was all she needed on top of everything else. She was just thankful that John had been persuaded to stay in his bed and that he was lying perfectly still with his eyes staring hopefully at the top of the stairs, waiting for her to check on him and maybe cuddle him too.

Hannah needed her nappy changing. That familiar buttery odour of wet nappy had been wafting around for a while but now it had been added to by that distinctive pong that could not be put off. Abigail held the baby tightly, both arms wrapped around Hannah, pinning the infant to her and preventing her from moving, as she went to get John out of bed. The nappies were downstairs and even if they were handy, she was going to have to heat some water on the stove to wash the mess away.

John obediently did as Abigail had asked and followed her to the top of the stairs, holding the bannister with one hand and holding out the other for his mother to guide him. He had been trained to come downstairs this way so he didn't tumble down them again. His legs always got tangled in his too long pyjama pants. They were hand-me-downs from a woman up the road but they kept John warm in bed and hopefully tomorrow she could find him some on the market that fitted a bit better. She could put the ones he was wearing away until he had grown a bit more, she thought absently.

Abigail shifted her daughter to free one arm so that she could guide her son downstairs. She was just about to take his hand when Hannah let out a long, piercing scream right into Abigail's ear. The shock caused Abigail to shout straight into Hannah's red, angry face.

"I have had enough! You will stop. I will make you stop. I cannot cope with you for a minute longer."

Then she lifted her daughter high above her head, ready to throw her down the stairs.

John was shouting. Why was John shouting Abigail thought? He never shouted. He was pointing. When Abigail followed to where he was pointing, she saw her daughter and realised what she had been prepared to do. Abigail, lowered the baby slowly and, shaking, she walked backwards into the bedroom until she felt the edge of the bedding box and sat down heavily.

****

Abigail stirred. What had disturbed her? Then as her eyes focussed, she saw Charlie standing over her. Her arms felt numb and she realised it was because she was gripping her children so tightly to her. Then she remembered. She had brought them both downstairs to sleep on the couch so that they were safe and secure in her arms. The shame of what she had been prepared to do coursed through her body and as she carefully moved each child, she stood and fell onto her husband's chest.

"Charlie, please forgive me. I am so sorry and I promise it will never happen again."   Abigail pleaded with her husband and as his arms enveloped her, she relaxed against him repeating over and over: "Never again, never again, never again".

Charlie was happy. He knew that Abigail was genuinely contrite and he made sure she could feel his power as he held her tightly. His arms were not exactly crushing her to him but his grip was tight enough so she squirmed. Yes, he thought. She is learning this wife of mine. She is improving and becoming what I expect her to be. His happiness turned to excitement as he felt a stirring in his groin.

"I forgive you my love. Now let me show you I have forgiven you." He led Abigail towards the stairs saying, "Hurry up before they wake up."

This was the last thing she wanted, but Abigail knew better than to refuse. He thought she had apologised for the row and as far as Abigail was concerned, that was how it would always be. She didn't dare think of the consequences if she told him what she was really sorry for doing.

Chapter 4.

Today was the day that Abigail had waited for. It was the day that Hannah would be hers forever. A proper daughter for her to raise. Abigail had grown to love this child who was crawling, laughed often and spoke more words and more importantly was now sleeping every night. It had been such a struggle in those early days but now Abigail could completely forget that she had contemplated hurting this funny, cute little girl who loved to please her and Charlie.

The memory of that dreadful night was fading and she had not had those vivid nightmares of throwing Hannah away from her so that she could have peace, the nightmare where the baby was bouncing off each wooden stair, and landing onto the concrete floor silently, for a while now. It was so peculiar, the nightmare. Abigail never saw blood on her daughter in this dream. She only saw eyes staring from the face of the little body that was so still. Not Hannah's beautiful blue eyes, but cold grey eyes of her birth mother. She always woke with such a start and Abigail was sure she had heard the voice of the woman who had brought Hannah into the world. The same words woke her every time and seemed to be filled with hatred.

"You promised me you would keep her safe. You are a liar".

Thankfully, the nightmare only happened when Charlie was on nights and she found herself waking up, crying and shaking, unsure if it was more than a dream. She could only calm down once she had made sure that Hannah was safely asleep in her cot but sleep always eluded Abigail for the rest of the night.

Abigail was over the moon to think that in a few hours she would have a legal document that meant no one could ever separate them.

Hannah Theresa Hennessey.

A proper name.

A name of substance.

A name of standing,

A name that was legitimised by a judge.

Even knowing that her daughter had been left a small piece of her birth mother with her middle name as a memento didn't dull Abigail's happiness. Hannah would have no reason to know of her first mother's lifelong gift and the promise made by Abigail in that disgustingly horrible place they had saved *her* daughter from.

The law stated that once a child was adopted, they would never be able to find their blood relations and Abigail was grateful for this. She couldn't bear the thought of Hannah finding her real mum and felt safe knowing that the law was on her side. Abigail had protection whilst this law was in place and she was convinced that it would never be changed. She would never let this child go from this day on. Abigail would make sure that Hannah was always a part of her life until the day she died. She would make sure that Hannah was always steered away from any information that would make her curious and tell her that her that being adopted didn't matter.

They had been advised by the social worker to make sure Hannah was aware that she was special and knew she was adopted as soon as they had the document that decreed this child was theirs and theirs only. This way, the social worker said, Hannah would just accept adoption as a normal part of her life and they would not have to worry about problems when the child was grown up. The child would just get used to hearing it. The only thing that Abigail was duty bound to tell Hannah was that the woman who brought her into the

world had tuberculosis at that time. But this was years away and only needed to be passed on if Hannah was pregnant so that they could keep an eye on the baby. Abigail had agreed but hoped that if that day came, medical breakthroughs had occurred and there was no need to
raise the subject. After all, new things were being brought into the NHS so quickly these days.

In a few hours they could choose what they told Hannah about her beginning of life. For Abigail, the less information that was shared about that, the better. She wanted to paint a picture of a perfect new start in life for a special little girl who they were delighted to have as their own. They had chosen her above all other babies to have their love and attention. This would show the child how much she was wanted and fitted with Abigail's need to be a whole woman. This little girl was her saviour from a life of denying she was inadequate. It made it easier as this was what Charlie wanted too, the perfect family befitting of his ideal life, even though adoption was, for him something that he would have preferred not to do.

"Anyway, the name Theresa is also my middle name" Abigail said to her reflection in the mirror that was propped up in the kitchen windowsill. "I will tell Hannah that I chose it for her and she will love me more for it."

Abigail began to free the rollers from her hair, pleased at the tight curls that bounced neatly in rows as she removed each one in turn, knowing that her hair would look pretty once
it was combed and teased into a mass of waves that would last all day as long as she put on plenty of lacquer and that Charlie would be happy with her appearance.

****

It had taken six months to get to this point of finalising the adoption for Hannah who was now only two months off celebrating her first birthday. It had been such a wait for the Hennesseys and for the first three months of having Hannah live with them, they knew that she could be taken into care unless the courts agreed to dispense with finding Lizzie Brady's missing husband. If the court decided that he had to be found, then they would lose Hannah and she would be taken into care as an abandoned child.

They had both been so relieved when they had been told that as long as Hannah's birth mother swore an affidavit in the courts that her daughter was illegitimate, nothing to do with her missing husband, was definitely the product of another man, her fault alone and that she didn't want to keep this infant, then the adoption process would go ahead. Charlie and Abigail were delighted when they were told it had been done and the wheels of protocol and procedure relating to adoption began to turn, albeit very slowly in their favour.

Now that this first bit had been dealt with, they had to wait for the Church to apply for an application of adoption order, which meant that Hannah was still classed as a child at risk and was under the care of The Liverpool Catholic Children's Protection Society. Charlie and Abigail knew that as long as the social workers' report on how they were looking after Hannah passed the expected level of care, that all the boxes were ticked as adequate, then they were on the last part of the journey of Hannah being made theirs.

The scrutiny was relentless and Abigail heaved a huge sigh of relief when they were informed of the court date to finalise and legalise their daughter's future with them. This could have been so different for all of them, she thought, but now her actions towards Hannah of a few months ago did not matter. Nothing mattered to Abigail as long as they got that certificate that proved she was a mother. A boy and a girl. The perfect family that she had wanted for so long.

The appointment for their hearing had been set for half past ten and Charlie had insisted that they got there half an hour early. This gave them more than enough time he said, to get to where they had to go without rushing. Charlie knew what he was talking about, thought Abigail and she was more than happy to let him organise the day. After all, he was experienced at going to court even if it was to give evidence against those who had done
wrong and he had arrested. It made her feel safe knowing he was such a pillar of the community. She looked at him with pride shining from her eyes as he carried Hannah in one arm and held John's hand and took the children into the building.

Abigail gaped as she walked in behind her husband and children. The main entrance led to a flight of stairs that took you to a massive first floor marbled entrance hall, which Charlie said was called the Court Ante-Room. It stretched out so far and had columns that were decorated with ornate green leaves that complemented the creamy coloured marble she noticed was also on the wall. There were gilded medallions on the wall showing profiles of men through history who had upheld the law and gave a sense of great importance to this place. Charlie pointed out the courtrooms and the entrance to the public gallery where some people spent hours watching and listening to the fate of others that was decided, ultimately, by a judge. Some people, he said, brought a flask and sandwiches and stayed all day, not because they were really interested, but because they were warm in here and it saved money on heating their own homes. Coal was not cheap and it eked out the money for a few days longer.

They stood together outside one of the doors and Abigail could feel her nerves getting the better of her. It was too

warm in this building and she was feeling sick. The heat seemed to
be coming from the floor and when she mentioned it to Charlie, he told her that the building had, in fact, got underfloor heating. Abigail was quite impressed with this fact but she wished it would all get started and they could soon leave and get fresh air.

Hannah was whining and wriggling to be put down so Charlie thrust the little one towards his wife and told her to keep Hannah quiet. Abigail lowered Hannah to the floor, holding her hands and helping her to stand. The child smiled happily and stamped her tiny feet and the floor echoed to the tapping sound she was creating. People passing by smiled at her antics and were more than happy to return the greeting of hello that Hannah offered to anyone who showed her attention.

Suddenly the door they were standing by opened and they were ushered into an impressive room with panelled walls, seating and a large desk. The judge instructed them to sit and gazed at the children. He seemed to be captivated by Hannah and smiled warmly at her as she stared intently at him before grinning and waving her arms at him.

Abigail didn't really get much chance to follow the proceedings, as she was too busy making sure Hannah was occupied, but could pick up enough to realise everything was going
well and in what seemed like minutes, she was being congratulated for officially becoming the mother of Hannah Theresa Hennessey and was being wished all the best for the future.

Chapter 5.

Hannah was two years and ten months old and was talking so fluently and easily. She was into everything and her incessant chatter was draining. She had to be answered and acknowledged as she soaked up information and demanded to know what every new thing she saw was called. Then she would repeat the word and insist that you looked as she pointed out her latest piece of learning.

At times, Abigail just couldn't stop what she was doing and indulge her daughter. It was impossible as she had a routine to follow and no matter what else she would like to be doing, she knew that Charlie would be checking to make sure everything was done to his high standards as soon as he came in from work. Abigail was always being admonished for the messy parlour, even though it wasn't really mess but just a few toys that the children had been playing with and the odd plate that was left from Hannah's and John's afternoon snack.

The only time Hannah was quiet and still was when she had paper and a crayon to play with or had her story books in which she delighted in pointing to the pictures and repeating the names of the animals that she could see. Hannah seemed to be lost in her own little world when she had a book, so Abigail had soon figured out that this was the ideal time to get a rest
before they set out to get John from school, or if she fancied a sit down and a cuppa with her neighbour.

Hannah had been kept quiet this way for most of the morning as Abigail was struggling to keep on top of almost any household tasks. She kept feeling dizzy and had been like this for a few days, but today, it seemed really bad. She kept feeling as though she needed to wee a lot too but when she went to the toilet, she couldn't pass a drop. She had nearly fallen over twice as the dizziness enveloped her and had decided to sit still for as long as she could and then hopefully, she would have recovered enough to make lunch. If she was no better tomorrow, she would go to the doctors, she thought. It might be something to do with John being poorly with mumps a few weeks ago and she hoped she wasn't starting with that.

Charlie was due home for lunch in half an hour and Abigail knew he would be angry with her if there was nothing ready for him as soon as he walked through the door but she was scared to stand up in case she collapsed completely. Hannah was crying and dragging at her to stand up but when she stood, Abigail felt as though every ounce of strength had left her body and she managed to get as far as the settee before she had to sit down.

"Go and fetch your book and we will read stories," she said to Hannah. "You can sit next to me and tell me stories until Daddy gets in for lunch".

Her daughter obliged and sat next to her. As she pointed to pictures of dogs and told her mother about Rex, the dog that lived next door, she was unaware that Abigail had passed out.

When Hannah did look at her mother, the child thought Abigail was asleep and quietly slipped off the couch. It was naughty to waken Daddy if he was asleep on the couch, so it would be naughty to waken Mummy too. Daddy shouted big at Mummy when Hannah did this and Hannah didn't like the shouting. Mummy always looked sad when Daddy shouted. Then mummy said she was naughty and it made Hannah sad and scared too.

****

Abigail knew she was awake but felt that her eyes would not open. She had no idea where she was and her head was pounding. She had been dreaming just before she woke and she could remember almost everything about it. It had been strangely peaceful, that dream, and she had felt as if she was watching it all unfold from high up, somehow detached from her body that lay very still below her and was bathed in light. She had told someone who was standing over her body that she wasn't ready.

It was at that point, the light faded and she had woken. Abigail had no understanding of the dream and as her consciousness grew, the start of the dream was hard to remember. It was almost as though she was not supposed to remember it but instinct told her that it was important. No doubt it would come back to her in the fullness of time.

Lying very still, she became aware of noises. Talking, music, something that sounded like a pram being pushed over cobbles, the rattling of the wheels as they bounced unevenly with each turn. Muted noises that made no sense to her.

She knew that she wasn't in her own bed. This one was hard on her back, not like the one she shared with… with who? Abigail knew she was married, so why could she not remember who she was married to? The children. There were two of them. Abigail and Stephen? No that wasn't right. What on earth where they called? Then she felt her body beginning to sag further into the mattress and all thoughts of names and the strange noises vanished as she fell into a deep sleep once again.

****

"Mrs Hennessey, it's nice to see you awake after all this time".

Abigail had no idea who was talking to her and smiled weakly at the man in a white coat who stared intently at her.

"You are in hospital, Mrs Hennessey and have been really poorly. You have been in a coma for quite a while, but now you have come around, we can get you better and before you know it you will be on your way home to your husband and two beautiful children".

Then he turned to the nurse who accompanied him and instructed her to go and telephone Mr Hennessey with the good news.

"Oh, by the way, I am Mr Phillips one of the consultants who works here in Clatterbridge Hospital. Now, we will start to do some tests and see how you get on later this afternoon, but for now, I just want you to lie still and not worry about anything. Your husband is on his way and will be here very soon. Once he gets here, we will have a chat about getting you up and about".

Abigail thanked this man and as he walked away wondered who was looking after the children. Her mind began to race and as panic set in, she started shouting for a nurse. What had happened to her? How long had she been here? Hannah and John – where they all right? As she tried to sit up, the nurse who had come to her aid gently encouraged her to lie still and
held her hand as tears cascaded down this poorly woman's cheeks, telling her that all would be well, it might take time, but all would be well.

Charlie had arrived and Abigail heard him before she saw him. As he came into view, followed by a nurse who was almost running to keep up with him, Abigail laughed as Charlie strode purposely towards her with the nurse demanding he was quiet and making much more noise than him in the process. Abigail decided to add to the chaos and shouted to him, "I'm here Charlie! I'm back in the land of the living and I'm here".

Encephalitis was rare. It was an infection that affected the brain and depending on which part of the brain it attacked, could be fatal. The parts it had affected would be forever damaged and Abigail felt blessed that this virus had died before it had taken her life. She was a cause of great interest to the trainee doctors and enjoyed talking with them and answering their many questions. She felt important and was happy to have them learn from her. They had been told not to tell her that being in contact with someone who had had mumps or other diseases such as chicken pox could cause it. Her son had recently recovered from a really bad bout of mumps and Abigail had nursed him back to health. They were convinced that this was the cause of it. Charlie had been told this and had insisted his wife never knew.

Abigail and Charlie had no idea of the long-term effects that this virus could cause and were both just grateful that she was on the mend. The doctors were delighted with her progress and Abigail had begun to feel much better. They were still concerned about her brain capacity as some days Abigail was quite forgetful and almost like a girl of fifteen in her outlook, but she could read, write, add money and her body had no paralysis. Anyway, the forgetfulness only lasted for a minute or so as far as Abigail was concerned and only happened if she nodded off during the day and it didn't matter to her at all as she always remembered eventually.

The main thing that this illness had affected was her bladder, but Mr Phillips had told her that once she reached the peak of her recovery, she would find ways to manage her bladder problems and would go on to live a normal life. That was how it had all started, Abigail thought as she remembered the day it had happened, when she could not pass water for love nor money and felt so poorly. She hoped that Hannah had not been too scared but Charlie said she was fine so that day didn't matter either.

Mr Phillips also added that, later today, the catheter would be removed permanently as she had now got the urge to pee back and needed to do exercises to strengthen her bladder. She was getting stronger by the day and her wasted muscles had started to recover, allowing her to walk a little further with each new day that dawned. Her whole being ached to get out of here and back to her family. Back to the way things were, she thought happily, blissfully unaware that this could ever happen.

Abigail knew that the children were being well cared for. Her mother had come to stay to look after them all. She was keeping everything running smoothly and the children loved her so much and were being really good, Charlie told her when she asked. Yes, John asked for his mummy often, she was told, but Hannah was too little to understand and was just happy to repeat that her mummy was in hospital and would be home soon, when she heard her brother asking or anyone mentioned Abigail.

This was not quite the truth, but Charlie couldn't bring himself to tell his wife that Hannah had been awful from the moment they carted Abigail off in the ambulance. Hannah had refused to be with anyone but him and cried if he was out of sight. In fact, she screamed the house down. She had stopped eating and getting her to sleep was a never-ending battle. The little mite had stopped talking for a few weeks too and apart from screaming, "I want my mummy!" she would not utter another word. Charlie was so relieved when Hannah began to eat and talk again and had accepted her Grandma as her caregiver. As usual, John had just got on with it and Charlie was happy to think that their son was not really affected. Not like Hannah by any means.

Abigail's mother was doing a great job but looking after Hannah and John was so hard and the woman was exhausted if truth be known. Charlie wanted to do more at home but he had to work and was struggling too, not only with the constant tiredness, but financially. He wasn't working nights and the bonus was a huge miss. He had borrowed money from Abigail's brother to tide them over until she was home and things went back to how they had been. Although Abigail's brother was more than happy to help and could afford the loan easily, Charlie hated being beholden to him.

Charlie knew that it would always be different, not as it had been. The doctor had said as much. He said that her mental capacity was limited and hopefully she would be able to do basic things like housework, looking after the children and maybe in time, work in jobs that were repetitive and needed no thinking about. As much as she looked and sounded normal, damage had been done.

He had hated asking for anything from anyone as Charles Hennessey felt he was failing in his duty to provide for his family. It was a painful reminder of days long ago, days when he had to beg, steal and borrow to keep his siblings fed and warm. He had his pride, had Charlie, and he felt as though his reputation and standing were diminishing before his very eyes.

He resented Abigail for being ill for so long. He resented the fact that his wife had managed to get an illness that left her mentally handicapped. It was not bad enough to have her put away, but it was still a handicap and he was furious to think he was saddled with this for the rest of his days. This was not how he wanted it to be. It was not part of his plan. Charlie wanted to run. He wanted to be anywhere but in this situation. His wife had failed him and his dreams were shattered. Charlie knew that he would just have to get on with it until the day came that the children were old enough to fend for themselves and then he was off out of it all.

The Inspector at the police station had given him a week off to organise things for the children and Abigail's family had rallied round immediately. At first, apart from Hannah, things were not too bad. Neighbours had helped and brought meals to the door and had taken John to school. Everyone in the police station had shown great concern and there had been a whip-round to help with travel costs so that Charlie could visit his wife once a week.

Charlie was embarrassed to take the kindness that was shown from others on face value. He felt that he was being pitied and was only just able to thank people for their generosity but hated having to do so. He was now fully in control and was managing perfectly well since his mother-in-law had arrived and he wanted no more handouts.

His blunt dismissal had offended people but Charlie didn't care. It was how he wanted it to be so that folk wouldn't get to know what was wrong with his wife. If she looked normal and sounded normal then that was what he needed the outside world to see. He would make sure that happened and tell everyone she was completely well when she came out of hospital. Abigail Hennessey would never know his plan and he was prepared to wait until Hannah was ready to leave school and he could put that plan into action. Thirteen years. Not long in the bigger scheme of things, mused Charlie. Thirteen. Unlucky for some, but not for him.

****

Abigail had been in hospital for six long months and today was the day that she was being discharged. Her husband was collecting her after lunch and that fitted nicely as she had time to say goodbye to everyone who had cared for her for all this time and as it was Wednesday, would get her final roast dinner served to her. The roasts were the best meals of the week and

Abigail looked forward to the tender roast pork, crispy roast potatoes, fresh vegetables and silky gravy that was on the menu today and got piled high onto her plate. Whatever would she eat on Sunday, she thought? The catering team at the hospital did a cracking roast chicken dinner followed by a hot pudding. Sunday tea was wonderful, as they had trifle and Abigail was partial to a good helping of trifle. She was going to miss that.

Charlie was escorting his wife off the ward, carefully holding her arm and making a great fuss of the staff, thanking them for their kindness and dedication in getting his wife better.

Abigail had decided to visit the toilet just before they left the ward and Charlie smiled as a nurse came out of the sluice room with a bowl of water, a towel and an arm full of clean sheets. She was going to wash a patient who had vomited and make them feel fresh, clean and respectable before visiting began. The young trainee nurse blushed furiously as Mr Hennessey winked saucily at her and said that she could give him a bed bath any time she wanted or if she fancied teaching him, he would be happy to practice on her. Charlie laughed as the slip of a girl walked quickly away from him, her head bent in embarrassment and she dropped the sheets in her panic to get as far away as possible from this horrible man. Charlie was just about to go over to the nurse and carry on his unwanted advances when Abigail returned and wanted to know what he was laughing at. As they passed the trainee, Charlie absently told his wife that he was amused by some useless trainee who couldn't keep hold of

couple of sheets. God help the patients when she had to carry them anywhere Charlie said meanly. If she dropped them, now that would be really funny.

Abigail stared in horror at her husband. What a dreadful thing to say! Abigail had made some good friends on this ward and her husband's comments had shocked her to the core. Charlie knew that most of these people she has spent the last six months with would never walk another step in their lives without help or if at all. Every patient, apart from her relied on the staff who helped every single one of them tirelessly and with love and care to move by being lifted bodily. The ward was solely for those who had caught Polio and were now suffering with paralysed legs. Because Abigail's illness was so rare and she needed constant care she had been placed here at her most critical point and had stayed here until this day. She was so grateful for her care and had presumed Charlie felt the same way. "Let's go home Charlie, I didn't find your comment funny and think it's time we left".

Charlie said he was only joking and when he glared at her, Abigail instinctively knew things between them had changed, and not for any good reason. If it wasn't for the children, she would have gone to live with her mother. Whatever her illness had left her lacking, it had also changed her husband from a domineering man into a monster. Abigail knew she was on borrowed time and that her mother-in-law's words would come true.

Chapter 6.

It sounded like a gunshot. It ricocheted in her head, a sound amplified that caused actual pain and she felt as though her ears were about to explode. Her hands instinctively went upwards and clamped over each one in an attempt to ease the pain and block out the high -pitched scream.

Abigail felt numb. She had waited for this moment for months. To be back home and to hold her son and daughter. To see them, to hug them to her and to take over the reins of motherhood from her own mother now that she was better.

As the numbness wore off and the pain and noise subsided, Abigail stood staring at her daughter. Hannah's arms were clamped around her grandmother's neck and the toddler was sobbing. "Not want you. Want Ganma. You go way!" Hannah buried her face into her grandma's shoulder and refused to look at her mother.

Abigail choked back her own tears and rubbed her hand over her cheek. It was stinging from the little hand that had delivered the slap. It was a slap so intense and unexpected that it
took Abigail completely by surprise and took her breath away. So much so, she was unaware of her son tugging at her arm, desperate to be acknowledged.

Charlie had stood, watching this scene unfold and he felt sorry for his wife. He had been wrong to upset her as they left the hospital and no matter how much he had apologised; Abigail had refused to forgive him. But this, this reaction from their daughter was worse than anything he had said. He had seen his wife physically recoil from their daughter and knew she was fighting to keep her composure.

"John wants you Abigail. Look, here's your big brave boy waiting to give you a hug and a present to say welcome home". He swept the boy off his feet and thrust him into Abigail's arms, hoping that she would turn her attention to him and that their son would defuse the situation.

Abigail instinctively put her arms out. As she felt her son's little body melt to her and his arms snake around her neck, she drank in the smell of his hair and felt the warmth of his hand that had reached to caress the redness of her cheek and she felt the tears roll down her cheeks.

"Mummy's home now and she won't go again. All will be well now. In time, all will be well," she whispered into the blonde wavy hair, looking over his head towards Hannah and hoping that her daughter would soon accept her again. If the mutinous look on Hannah's face was anything to go by, Abigail knew she had a fight on her hands and prayed silently for all the holy saints to help her daughter and give her, Abigail, strength for yet another battle with this child.

John stared intently at his mother, his eyes roaming over every inch of her face as though he was unable to believe she was here. Her quiet boy relieved to have her back, smiled at Abigail as she lowered him gently to the floor. Then silently, John took his mother's hand and led her to where his present for her was waiting.

Charlie took Hannah from his mother-in-law. He pulled his daughter roughly from the arms that had held and protected her for the last few months and despite the screams of protest from the girl, carried her to where Abigail and John were sitting. As he dumped Hannah unceremoniously onto the floor by her mother's feet, Charlie's voice startled everyone into silence as he bellowed, "Hannah Theresa Hennessey! Shut up now!"

Then he walked into the garden and picking up the spade began to dig frantically at the border he was preparing for flowers, only stopping when his tears blinded him. He swiped them away with the back of his hand wishing he could swipe himself away as easily as his tears. He wished that he could rub over the crumbling picture of his life and swipe away the last six months that had turned his dreams to dust.

****

Abigail was sorting out the children's toys. They hadn't had many before, but since she had come out of hospital, she had noticed that there were more. Abigail's brother had been to visit and had taken the children to a toyshop for a treat. Although she didn't mind the children being spoiled, a lot of the new toys made noise and she couldn't stand the incessant hooting of the fire engine horn or the high-pitched squeak that emanated from a family of ducks when they were squeezed. They were meant to be for the bath, but Hannah liked to play with them downstairs. She would sing that song about a mummy duck saying quack, quack, quack and mix her numbers up as to how many ducklings returned to their mother.

It went on and on and Abigail's patience was wearing thin. The noise gave her a headache and made her ears hurt. There was only one thing for it. Abigail would remove the noise making parts tonight when the children were asleep and Charlie was on nights. Abigail could hear a pin drop since she had been ill and at times it was a blessing, but at other times, it was a curse. The curse was that she could hear a conversation from yards away and although she enjoyed the odd bit of gossip and was able to tell Charlie of any wrongdoing that she overheard that broke a law, she was mortified when she heard something that was about her.

Abigail had walked into the grocers. There were a couple of women who went to the church that Abigail took the children to every Sunday and they were discussing the tally man and his frequent visits to the police house on Mill Dam Lane. Always on the same days, they were telling the shopkeeper, always in the afternoons. Someone had seen him go in. Yes, right inside *and* through the front door *and* Lady Muck didn't even bother to see if anyone noticed. No, they really were not sure if it was every week, but anyway, it was disgusting to think that the wife of a man of such standing could do such a thing. It was obvious her husband was at work as that police motorbike wasn't on the drive and that spoke volumes.

Yes, that's what they had been told. A man in a suit. It had to be the repro or the tallyman. They were the only ones who wore suits. It was because of their need to look like authority, one of the women said when the shopkeeper asked if she was sure.

Well that's what they had heard, the second women stated, nodding her head to make her point fully.

Well, said the first woman, all that new furniture had to be paid for somehow and laughed raucously, implying that the reason for the tallyman's visits was obviously related to payment not in money but in kind.

As Abigail walked towards the counter, the shopkeeper coughed and rather too loudly announced, "Good morning Mrs Hennessey, it's lovely to see you. And how is little Hannah? Full of beans as usual? I will just finish serving these two ladies and then sort you out". He pushed his hand into a jar on the counter and pulled out a lollipop. As he handed it to the child, he smiled warmly as Hannah grinned and said, "Ta man".

The two women grabbed their shopping bags when they realised the focus of their gossip had walked in the shop and tried to escape but Abigail knew that she had to nip this in the bud.

"Yes, you are right, ladies, the tallyman did call twice in one a week. He called for payment for all the beautiful furniture that my husband ordered, that is in keeping with his profession and reflects his standing in this community and that, from your comments, you are very aware of. Oh, and just so you know on the first visit, he discussed with my husband a family who had robbed him of his takings, a family from this very town who are now looking at a visit to Court. The second day was with an updated payment card and with some paperwork for my husband to read over. Then he went with my husband into the back garden to look at the so-called missing motorbike and help him fix the side mirror back into place. The very bike that has been there for over a week as someone keeps damaging it if it's left on the drive. Anyway, I will tell my husband you have been asking after him when he gets home. He will be delighted to know that you have such a keen interest in our lives. He will, no doubt, want to call to see you to find the name of your source of such rich information and thank them personally."

The two women, who had been blushing furiously, suddenly lost that red hue and their faces went white. Both looked shocked and a bit scared by this woman's comments, Abigail grinned at the shopkeeper and reached into her basket for the shopping list she had made so that she wouldn't forget anything.

The women beat a hasty retreat. If Mrs Hennessey's husband did call on them then they needed to say the same thing to their respective husbands and to try to lessen the backlash that would be meted out once the police had left each house. To have the local bobby call was not acceptable, even less acceptable when it was gossip that had caused it.

Hadn't they both been admonished by the Priest while their men stood by them and found out about them and their gossiping ways only last Sunday, for speaking ill of people? Both women had been rounded on harshly and had promised their husbands it wouldn't happen again.

There were not many in this town who liked PC Hennessey but he had to be shown respect because of his job and they had seen and heard of others who had interfered with his private life being dealt with swiftly and quite unmercifully.

He was a dark horse, this policeman, and people in this town, who were close knit and curious in nature would take any opportunity to find something to discuss about those who they classed as different. Everybody discussed everyone's business but then, most were related anyway so that was expected, but these two housewives knew that they had gone too far. They got out onto the road as quickly as they could, not even stopping to answer Hannah as she shouted "Bye yaydies" through a mouth full of the sweet, sticky lollipop.

That was close, Abigail thought and was aware of a slight tremor in her hand as she put the piece of paper onto the counter. If only they knew the truth. Abigail hoped that that was something that would never be discovered and patiently waited for the shopkeeper to get her goods. It was bad enough that most of the women of this town thought Abigail was a snob
because she kept herself to herself as Charlie demanded and the last thing that she wanted from any of them was their false pity or ridicule if the truth got out.

As Abigail paid for her shopping and persuaded Hannah it was time to go, she had never felt as lonely and alone as she did at this moment.

Wearily, she walked with her daughter back to the house that was anything but a happy family home and wondered sadly, if it would ever be happy again. She had lied to protect her husband's reputation and was amazed at how easily she had done this. "Learning from my master", Abigail mumbled as she ran and grabbed Hannah's hand before the child ran into the road.

She unlocked the back door that led into the kitchen and walked slowly into the parlour, Abigail stared forlornly at Charlie's shirt. He hadn't noticed the smear on his collar and when Abigail had confronted him, Charlie had lied through his teeth until she said she was going to see Inspector Cross because she couldn't cope with any more. Abigail had said she was going to take the children and stop with her mother until she was sure he was prepared to make amends and change his ways.

"You don't deserve us, so you can't have us," Abigail had stated quietly and left Charlie in a right panic.

It wasn't until his boss had called to the house that Abigail had found out the full reason why Charlie was given an extra week's leave out of the blue and he could no longer lie about the shirt. Once Inspector Cross had been, that was when Charlie had left. He needed space to sort himself out, he had told Abigail and once he had decided, he would let her know what was to happen.

Abigail wished that it *had* been the tallyman who visited twice in one week and that the story she had given those two women was the truth as she cut the shirt that Charlie Hennessey had worn, the night before his impromptu holiday began, into pieces with pinking shears. As the blades sliced through the material it was as though each cut reached her heart that beat in time to the words from her marriage vows, "For better, for worse", until she collected up all the pieces and threw them onto the glowing embers of the coal fire.

She stood, motionless, as the embers popped and sizzled into life and tiny flames that engulfed every fibre burned away last shreds of her composure. Abigail stared at the dying flames and she began to cry.

Chapter 7.

As the tears streamed down Abigail's face, she wondered how could life change so quickly. She spoke to the fire, her voice low and sad.

"It's so unfair. I knew that my suspicions from weeks back might lead to this point. I had been right and I feel so foolish for believing my husband, Mr Charlie bloody cheating Hennessey. He *has* been seeing another woman and now what is going to happen to my marriage, home or Charlie?"

She began to relive every moment that had led her to burning her husband's shirt knowing it would be of no use, unable to stop the events playing over and over until she was numb.

It had started a month ago.
That was the first time she had seen it.
When she had picked his shirt up off the bedroom floor Abigail had noticed a lipstick stain on the collar and a smaller stain on the shoulder. Abigail had been terrified to ask Charlie about the marks. If he was seeing another woman, she would rather not know. She had
washed his shirt and scrubbed the collar until every trace had gone. Then she promptly told herself it didn't matter and carried on as though she had not seen anything.

When it happened again, he had given her the excuse of a drunken woman throwing herself on his mercy as they arrested her husband for fighting in the Sun Inn. He was so believable as he described how this woman was like an octopus and he had had to restrain her and forcibly push her away. Her head had made contact with his shoulder, so that's when it must have marked his shirt, he said. Again, Abigail felt it better to accept the explanation as he said that it was all written in his police notebook and if she was so bothered, he would show her.

The third time, Abigail knew that something was not right. It was the same colour lipstick but this time she could see it had been more than a chance marking. When she confronted Charlie, he did eventually own up to having a fling.

Nothing but a bit of stupidity Charlie said. A woman who was available and he took a risk. It meant nothing to him and he had only seen her a couple of times. It was Abigail he was married to and that meant everything to him. His marriage and the children were so important and he had stated quite categorically that it was over with this woman. Abigail
calmly told him he was nothing but a cheating liar and all she had ever done was what he wanted and this was how she was repaid.

Then Charlie had implied it was Abigail's illness that had brought this fling about. A man had needs and until she was stronger, he had been generous enough to leave her alone. She should be grateful, he spat at her, as she had not been able to do what he wanted for months now. Then the row escalated and Abigail made sure that her voice matched his, shout for shout, loud enough for the neighbours to hear everything.

Abigail was hoping that if her neighbour, Sally Hall, knew anything, the row might prompt Sally to tell her. Abigail had to know who this woman was. She wanted to ask this woman if she had thrown herself at her husband and demand it stopped. If she ever saw the woman and it was found to be Charlie's doing, she would cope with that answer, if she ever got one, later.

Charlie never thought that his secret would lead to him being suspended, pending an inquiry into his behaviour as a police officer, from a row with his wife. He genuinely believed he could get this sorted with his wife and everything would go back to normal. He hadn't realised that his colleague PC Sam Hall, who lived in the adjoining police house, had
reported Charlie's behaviour towards his wife as he was worried about the children's and Abigail's safety. Sam also knew that Charlie Hennessey was having a fling, in fact it had been going on for so long it was now getting to the point that it had to be reported. It was a serious relationship and that was frowned upon. The police had to be upstanding, moral men and women and Charlie Hennessey was neither an upstanding or moral man.

This row couldn't have come at a better time as both the men were studying for a sergeant's post in the same station and there was only one position available. If he could get the cheating Charlie Hennessey out of the running, the job was more or less his. Every cloud, Sam thought as he kissed his wife goodbye and set off for the police station the very next morning.

****

Abigail had been told by Charlie that he had been given a week off to do some work in the house and to study for his sergeant's test that was due in a month or so. He couldn't have the motorbike at home. Rules, he said. Getting fixed, he'd added when she asked where it was.

He had casually asked her to make sure that the front room was spotlessly clean as the Inspector might be making a visit. Something to do with that fling Charlie had said. Abigail had nodded, unable to speak at the mention of the affair. The room just had to be done properly, and she had to keep the kids out once she had gone from top to bottom and it was up to his standards, Charlie had told her as he grinned and went to hug her. Abigail had stood perfectly still as the man she loved despite his infidelity, put his arms around her. It was too soon for Abigail to pretend everything was all right between them.

****

It was the kind of knock at the door that made you jump. An official knock. Like the knock of a policeman, Abigail thought as she walked down the hall to see who it was. She giggled as she realised that her Charlie must knock on hundreds of doors in this way. It made her proud to think of him having so much authority in his hands. He could make people take notice and she liked that despite all her marital problems that had blackened her world.

As she opened the door, Abigail realised she was looking at her husband's superior and the smile that was still playing around her lips vanished. The Inspector visiting was always a
rare occasion and Abigail quickly invited him in. She wondered what would be said but more importantly, what the end result would be.

"Please take a seat in the lounge, Sir. I will go and get Charles. If I had known you were visiting today, I would have baked. I hope a biscuit with your tea will be all right, oh, that's if you would like a cup of tea?"

The Inspector smiled kindly at this woman and told her that tea would be fine as he looked around the room, noticing the new furniture that was spotlessly clean. He wondered if these items would be in this room for much longer and as he sat, sighed wearily, knowing that his visit was going to cause upset to an innocent woman who was not fully aware of his reason for being in her home.

He had purposefully left this visit until he was off duty so he could take off his uniform and dress in trousers and a jacket. If the children happened to be around, he wanted them to see him as a person, not a policeman who was being strict with their father. He had told PC Hennessey to organise for a neighbour to have the children for an hour and hoped that his instruction had been followed. The girl was too young to understand but the boy would probably understand more and there was enough trouble in this house without him adding to it. The last time he had been here was when they had officially adopted the little girl and he came with gifts for both children to welcome and acknowledge that they were a family of four.

What a difference three years can make, he thought, as he listened for footsteps that would alert him to PC Hennessey's presence. He was hoping to have a word with Charles in private before his wife came in with the tray of tea. It would only take a minute but it was important.
He needed Charles Hennessey to know that he had done the same and had with hard work and a bit of change, still been successful in furthering his career to where he was today.
Inspector Cross hoped that this officer would see sense and not throw his career onto the scrap heap over some silly mistake.

****

Abigail's head was spinning. This could not possibly be right. This was not what Charlie had told her and even though she had struggled to accept his explanation and being blamed for her not being wife in every way, well, in the bedroom, she was struggling to comprehend what she was listening to.

Just stop was all she could think but didn't dare voice. If she made one noise, she felt that nothing more than a scream would come from her lips. She felt bereft but at the moment had to hold on. She could not show herself up in front of the Inspector and Charlie would be so angry at her letting him down.

What on earth was she thinking? It was obviously the opposite way around. Charlie had let her, the children and his boss down and she was still defending him. Abigail felt like she was a chattel. In fact, that's exactly what she was and had been for quite a while. The shame of it all was too much for Abigail to bear and she ran to the bathroom hoping she would not vomit before she reached the toilet.

****

"Now PC Hennessey, we need to find a way forward from this, this erm, happening that you have admitted to. I am here help you and want you to know that I have stuck my neck out for you and feel that it will be in everybody's best interests if you agree to what I am going to suggest," Inspector Cross stated. "Mrs Hennessey, this might be upsetting for you, but I have to make sure that you have the full picture as you too are involved in this decision and it will also affect the children. So, let's not waste time and see if we can get this sorted out so that
everyone benefits," he added, looking kindly at Abigail and wishing he was anywhere but in this room.

As Abigail began to listen, she felt as though she was in another world.

Charlie had been seeing his other woman for two years so it was no casual fling as he had made her believe. This was serious and Charlie was admitting to his boss that he had feelings for this woman. Deep feelings and he wasn't sure if he could let her go as he said he loved the woman.

Inspector Cross was angry and demanding Charlie saw sense. Charlie had a week to make his mind up. One week and he would be kept off work until he had an answer.

"You have a choice, PC Hennessey and the outcome will affect every area of your life, that of your wife and children, your role as a police officer and your living arrangements," Inspector Cross said levelly. "If you do not give this woman up, you will be disciplined and released from the force. In effect, you will have no home, no income, family life will end and you will be on the scrap heap. The chances of you getting a reference will be slim and the woman who you claim to be so enamoured with will have to support you and as our inquiry
into this affair has revealed, she is not in a position to do so," the man continued. "However, there is a solution. If you give up this woman and I mean never see her again, then your position as a Police Constable will be safe. It will mean that this incident is held on record and you will not be able to apply for promotion for a while. It will also mean that you will be transferred to another area sometime within the next year as long as we are satisfied that you have broken all contact and prove to be what is expected from a man of the law. One, just one whole week PC Hennessey, and I will be waiting for your answer. You are to report to me at the headquarters in Preston. I have written down the date and time and hope the answer you bring is in favour of your career, your wife and family".

As the Inspector stood to leave, he nodded to Abigail and said; "I hope we meet in better circumstances in the future Mrs Hennessey". Then glaring at Charlie, he stated, "You are a fool, don't become an even bigger fool. Do the right thing and keep your status intact."

Chapter 8.

January 1966 was the start of not only a new year but was also a milestone in Hannah's life. Abigail was walking her daughter to school for the first time and was feeling relieved that this day had come.

Hannah, who had just had her fifth birthday, was a very clever child and was into everything. Her insatiable appetite for learning was growing to the extent that Abigail would be glad to have a few hours peace and quiet from the incessant thirst for knowledge her daughter displayed. No more questions. Abigail was sick to the back teeth of listening to why, what and how. It irritated her that Hannah was not one to be happy with a short answer but needed more and more to satisfy this desire to learn and went on and on.

Abigail felt intimidated especially when Hannah demanded to know why she, her mother did not know an answer and this made Abigail feel so worthless that she controlled the situation by calling Hannah a naughty, rude little girl who was far too clever for her own good.

"Nobody likes children who are nosey and ask lots of questions and if you don't stop asking questions and talking all the time then you will have to have your tongue cut out to stop you talking once and for all and asking anything," Abigail told her daughter. "You can only ask questions in school and if you don't stop bothering me then I'll take you to the doctors to get it done tomorrow. Now get from under my feet and go and play with your toys."

The fearful look on the child's face made Abigail feel better in one way as she knew she would have no more trouble today and she sighed loudly as Hannah slunk away to get her doll and that disgusting shawl that was more holes than wool. On the other hand, Abigail felt awful as she knew that it was her own inability to manage her young daughter's insatiable appetite for knowledge and as much as she loved this child with all her being, it was wearing her out.

Abigail needed some aspirin as her head was pounding but at least with Hannah silenced, the pain would soon ease and then she would be able to cope with the rest of the day. Hannah would understand one day that her mummy was not always able to cope with day to day living and Abigail hoped that her daughter would always know that no matter what, she was doing the best she could.

Abigail shouted for Hannah to come to the table for a biscuit and a drink and the little girl dutifully did as she was told and climbed onto the chair ready to be given her snack. When Abigail spoke to Hannah, there was no answer offered and she realised that Hannah was staring at her with eyes full of tears.

"Don't you dare start crying or I will give you something to cry for and when I talk to you, you must answer me. Now eat your biscuit and drink all that milk and when you are finished you can play upstairs while I clean the bathroom before John gets in from school."

Abigail couldn't understand why her daughter wasn't speaking and looked so upset as she sat silently pushing the biscuit round the plate rather than eating it. It was when Hannah sniffed noisily that Abigail realised tears were running down Hannah's face.

"Stop crying this instant and get on with that snack." Abigail demanded as she glared at Hannah. "If you don't stop now, you will leave the table and I will smack your legs for being ungrateful and not eating what I give you. Stop crying now or get away from the table."

As Hannah couldn't stop crying, she decided it best to leave the table. As she slid from the chair her arm caught the cup with the milk in and it spilled over causing a puddle that began
to run towards the edge of the table. Abigail jumped up and dragged her daughter away from the river of milk and began to slap at Hannah's legs until the child was screaming.

"I told you I would give you something to cry for if you didn't behave yourself!" Abigail spat at Hannah. "Now look at the mess you have made, you are a naughty girl. Go and sit on that settee and don't move until I tell you to and stop that bloody din."

Abigail ignored her daughter in the hope that Hannah would stop crying but when it did not work, she began laughing at her and calling her 'lady tearful', mimicking the child unmercifully until Hannah begged her to stop and tried to hide in the corner of the settee, desperately wiping her tears onto the cushion and wondering if her Mummy would carry out her threat to have her tongue cut out.

Abigail was feeling guilty for treating her little girl so horribly but that child would test the patience of the Good Lord himself. Hannah had to learn that it was too much for Abigail to cope with when she was bombarded with noise all day. Her head hurt so much Abigail was sure that it was going to explode and she found it a struggle to concentrate and keep her temper in check. Maybe when Hannah was at school all day, Abigail would be able to
manage much better and not be as harsh with the child. Her head would not be sore because the house would be quiet.

****

As they walked, Hannah jumped, hopped and smiled incessantly. Her little face radiating happiness that Abigail had never witnessed in her daughter and this made her feel slightly angry. Hannah seemed to like to be with anyone but her and would laugh and chatter happily and it hurt Abigail deeply.

Ever since the incident with the milk, Hannah had been quiet but was much easier to manage all day and Abigail was coping much better too. Her daughter only cried if she fell over but would not let anyone see her tears and hurriedly wiped them away. It was strange, thought Abigail, how Hannah's face went blank and she clamped her lips together so tightly that they went white any time a tear rolled down her cheek.

"I hope the teacher can tire you out and not the other way around," Abigail said as she bent to tie the laces in Hannah's new school shoes. She laughed when her daughter replied that her teacher would have to have a sleep in the afternoon if that happened.

Abigail felt dreadful as they went through the school gate and Hannah shook her mother's hand away and began to run to the classroom door. As she shouted for her daughter to come and give her a kiss goodbye, Hannah turned and said "No. I'm a big girl now and kissing isn't allowed in school," and with that vanished into the building.

Why on earth has this child to be so wilful and independent? Abigail wondered as she stood watching other mummies prising their crying offspring from them. Her daughter never acted like these children, who seemed to have such a closeness to their parents. Abigail had tried everything to get Hannah to be more how she wanted her to be.

A proper daughter who wanted to be with her all the time.

A proper daughter who was happy to just fit in with her view on how Hannah should be.

Why did she have to ask questions that Abigail couldn't or refused to answer? Especially around adoption. Thankfully, Hannah seemed to have got the message that asking questions got her nowhere apart from into trouble now, very rarely asked anything apart from whether she could get a drink of water.

Abigail sometimes wished that they had never told Hannah about her adoption, that she had a mummy who could not care for her and that she was special because Abigail and
Charlie had chosen to make her their daughter. Hannah was too curious about all this and Abigail felt as though, given an opportunity in the future, her daughter would look for the woman who brought her into the world and demand answers. But at least Abigail was safe in the knowledge that this would never happen and that in time, Hannah would understand that she had not to ask or speak about her adoption to anyone.

It was upsetting and Abigail was not sure how she would manage if people found out that her daughter was illegitimate and that this was the only way they could have a family. Ah, well, she mused, at least John had been easy to deal with. He had also been told from an early age and Abigail sometimes wondered if her son had any idea what they were talking about. John just took it all in his stride, staring at her until she stopped talking and then going back to play with his cars, muttering to himself about petrol and driving very fast to find proper mummy.

Abigail sighed as she walked through the school gate and headed for home. A cuppa and a bit of toast would be most welcome when she got in. After that, she would have all the time in the world to do the housework without any interruptions. As her pace quickened, Abigail felt her spirits rise. It would do her and Hannah good to have some time

apart and anyway, it was the teacher's turn to put up with the never-ending questions. At least teachers got paid
for all that irritation and if Hannah carried on in school like she did at home, then no doubt the little girl would soon realise that a slap from a teacher hurt and she would behave herself and learn to be quiet in school too.

****

As she turned the corner onto Mill Dam Lane, Abigail's heart skipped a beat and she felt the hairs on the back of her neck stand up. Charlie's motorbike was on the drive and he should be at work. Fear gripped her as she walked to the back door and opened it slowly. She didn't dare think of what was wrong, of what she had done that was so bad to bring him home from work. Her stomach churned as she shouted, "Hello love, what brings you home early"? She hoped that her voice didn't waver and she sounded normal.

Charlie stood in front of the fireplace, hands behind his back, ramrod straight and with a face as dark as night. He glared at Abigail and told her to sit at the table. Once she was seated, she winced as his hand slammed down in front of her onto the plastic tablecloth and when he lifted his hand up, she saw a piece of paper with a list of food items and the prices of each one. They were all neatly written with a total at the bottom of the page.

Abigail was rooted to the chair and stared at the paper in disbelief. How on earth had he got this? The shopkeeper had promised her that he wouldn't tell her husband as long as it was paid by today. He said it was fine for her to pay it a week later as it was a five-week month and had agreed that she could call in with it on her way to pick Hannah up from school. He said that as long as she didn't get anything else on credit until this lot was cleared, she had nothing to worry about but he would have to be paid today.

"I've paid the newspaper bill today," Charlie said evenly. "Two bloody months' worth and for next week too so that we can still have them delivered. If that wasn't enough to fork out, I was also hit with this. Need to pay today, Mr Hennessey and really sorry but no more credit will be given, Mr Hennessey. Cash for all goods from now on, Mr Hennessey. What the bloody hell do you think you were doing Abigail? I give you more than enough money each month to keep house and I want to know what you are spending it on. It's obviously not on food."

He snatched the paper up from the table and waved it in front of her face. "I have never been as embarrassed in my life and I want an explanation now!" he shouted. Abigail nearly fell off the chair as he brought his face close to hers and he whispered, "Well? I'm waiting."

Abigail didn't know what to say. She knew whatever she said would be wrong so decided to keep quiet and hoped that Charlie would not lose his temper. She had tried to tell Charlie a few months ago that she was struggling to make the housekeeping stretch for a month and that when there was five weeks in a month, she really needed a bit more. Charlie had dismissed her request and said she would have to manage. He couldn't give her any extra money and that was the conversation closed. Food prices had been going up and Charlie was so fussy about what he ate. It had to be the most expensive cuts of meat, the branded foods that cost much more all because of a name, and he even insisted that she bought proper coffee that cost a king's ransom.

Charlie took her silence as an insult and Abigail watched in horror as he clenched his fist and drew his arm back. She closed her eyes and prepared herself for the pain that she would soon suffer from the vicious punch he was about to bestow. She was grateful that he would not mark her face but knew that her arm would be bruised and stiff to move for days. When the blow came, it was so hard that it knocked

Abigail from the chair. She lay perfectly still on the cold linoleum, hoping that she didn't pass out as her vision blurred and the ceiling started to spin.

As Charlie pulled her to her feet, Abigail vomited. Her husband's face turned ashen as he realised that she might be suffering from concussion and that he was the cause of it. Gently, he led her to the settee and helped her to sit down. He placed cushions behind her back to make her comfortable and told her to sit still.

"I'm so sorry Abigail. I didn't expect you to fall and hurt yourself. Did you bang your head when you slipped off the chair? You were sitting on the edge of that chair you know and you must have lost your balance. After all, I only tapped you to make you answer me. It wasn't like I actually hit you hard enough to make you fall. Now you sit quietly and I'll get you a cup of tea. If you feel sick again, just shout and I'll fetch you a bucket. Don't close your eyes and stay awake." Charlie was panicking but he knew better than to show it as he would have to admit it was his fault. Anyway, Abigail would forgive him. She always did and it would all be smoothed over in no time, especially when he told her she was going to get more money when there were five weeks in a month so that she could manage until she got a part time job now that Hannah was at school.

He would ask around for a small cleaning job for his wife from some of his well to do contacts even though in his mind it was a menial job for the lowest of the low. Charlie would say it was more for company as she was at a loose end now both the children were at school. A couple of mornings a week would do her just fine and she would still be able to run the home and see to the children as he demanded. Then he could reduce the housekeeping back
to the usual amount and have no more worries about being made to look like a poor fool by that jumped up shopkeeper.

Abigail smiled weakly at her husband as she settled back into the cushions, knowing that to answer him would fall on deaf ears. Charlie had made his mind up that he was not to blame for any of this and Abigail knew that she had to just get on with the day as though nothing had happened. If she told herself it didn't matter that her husband had hit her, she would soon be able to forget it had ever happened. Anyway, the general store in the village was still prepared to give her credit if she needed it, so as long as she paid the money back every Monday when she drew the family allowance, she would be fine.

Chapter 9.

Her fingers were sore. In fact, they were so painful that she could hardly hold the material in place to make the next stitch. The handle of awl she was using was taped up and she hoped that when Mr Thompson came to collect this month's order, he would have a new one for her. The needle kept moving and Abigail was pricking her fingers more than the soft sheep leather and it was taking her twice as long to produce any decent pieces.

Abigail had reluctantly agreed to work from home, cutting and sewing pieces of chamois leather together to form a mop head. She had to produce as many as possible from the huge bags of off cuts that were dropped off every fortnight along with the waxed thread. She was finding the work awkward and boring and struggled to cut each piece into a strip that was nine inches long by two inches wide and as straight as she could get it. The smell of the treated sheep hide was disgusting and Abigail was having to wash her hands for ages to get rid of the greasy feel and that sickly smell that suck to her skin like glue and that was making her fingers worse. The carbolic soap had dried her skin and her already damaged fingers were cracked, red raw and swollen to the point that she was struggling to bend them.

All this for ten bob thought Abigail as once again the needle on the awl moved and she winced from yet another stab. She was so far behind on this lot. Abigail knew she would have to work into the early hours of the morning to get the forty needed for the ten-shilling note that she could earn to keep her going until Charlie gave her the housekeeping.

Her husband had been true to his word and upped her allowed amount to cover the five-week months but it had come with another price tag. She had to work somewhere, anywhere and do anything to repay the shopping she had got on tick that Charlie had paid for and then once her debt was paid, she had to continue working if she wanted extra money for that extra week. When she was told about this chamois leather sewing, Abigail had decided to give it a go.

Working from home sounded ideal but that was far from the case. There was no money to find for bus fares, it would fit in with the children and the housework and Charlie's meals would be ready on time. Those were the good things. Abigail kept these thoughts to the front of her mind but the reality was totally different. The house smelled from the chamois leather and Abigail could not get to grips with making anything half decent. She had not had one full payment since she started this job and would have been more than happy to pack it in if she didn't have to repay Charlie. No matter how bad it was, Abigail knew she had to keep going and pretend that she was managing and had told her husband she enjoyed the work. It was therapeutic, she told Charlie. It helped her to focus. She said she was so sorry for the trouble she had brought him and would work hard to pay him back and make him happy with her again.

Of course, Charlie wasn't happy. He was not happy about the mess she made from the cutting and refused to let her work when he was home as he needed all the attention. She had got further behind with the order because he had been off work for a week with a bout of flu.
She had been run ragged by his demands of drinks, clean sheets every day because he wouldn't lie in a sweat drenched bed and the extra washing this created was getting on Abigail's nerves. She had to light the fire in the bedroom and run to put more coal on when he decided the room wasn't warm enough even though he was more than capable of getting out of bed and do it himself. Even when he was feeling better all he did was sit on the settee and demand that she sat with him, then complained when she got behind with the cleaning.

As the needle once again jabbed into her finger, Abigail threw the offending implement at the wall and with a sweep of her arm, cleared every bit of material onto the floor. "Will life ever get better?" Abigail muttered as she stared at her fingers and watched as blood dripped onto table until her vision was blurred by her tears.

Abigail stood at the back door smiling warmly at Mr Thompson and thanked him over and over. It wasn't often that she was lucky, but today was definitely lucky in more ways than one.

Mr Craig Thompson, or Craggy as he was often called, looked embarrassed as he tried to make his way out of the house with two huge sacks of chamois leather cuttings as well as the bag with the completed order of forty mops. He had decided to give Mrs Hennessey an extra two shillings as she had, after all, kept to her part of the bargain despite not having the best of tools to work with. He admired this woman's determination and if truth be known, felt sorry for her. That husband of hers didn't treat her right and he had heard about the shop incident.

It was his brother, Jimmy, who owned the shop and after that policeman had left after settling the debt, Jimmy had mentioned how worried he was about Mrs Hennessey's safety. The copper looked like he was going to commit murder when he left, his brother had said.

Jimmy wished with all his heart he had waited for Mrs Hennessey to pay up but that interfering wife of his had seized this opportunity to cause trouble and give the other people in the shop a bit of juicy gossip to chew over when she said about the outstanding paper bill. Then when she realised that she had an audience, she added to his embarrassment by
demanding Mr Hennessey paid the credit as well. It had done his business the power of good though, as all the other

women who had goods on credit came and settled their accounts on the agreed day as not one of them wanted their husbands to be humiliated and to have to suffer the backlash. If the shopkeepers could treat a policeman like that, they didn't dare think about how their husbands would be treated and some of the women had actually paid early and asked for the amount of tick they could have weekly to be reduced to a more manageable amount.

Craggy had been unsure about being so closely linked to the policeman as everyone in the small town thought he was a nasty piece but he had agreed to give Mrs Hennessey the work when she said it was only for a month or two.

He had an inkling that this Hennessey woman was being made to work by that husband of hers and if it helped to make things easier for her and the children, it was, in one way, the right thing to do. There was a rumour that Hennessey had broken his wife's arm over the tick money she had owed and he didn't like that kind of thing happening to a woman. Yes, he slapped his own wife on occasion but it never did her any harm and he would never make a mark show on his wife. That would be wrong, he thought. Not only that, but he was struggling to find people to work for him and he had a big order to fulfil. As he saw it, Mrs Hennessey was a means to an end to benefit him and keep him in business but local people would think he was a kind-hearted man helping out this downtrodden woman. It was a win-win situation that he couldn't pass by.

As he walked as quickly as he could to his van, Craggy breathed a huge sigh of relief that he had been able to make a break from this woman. He had never been as pleased to hear anything in his life when Mrs Hennessey said they were being transferred to a new area and couldn't do any more work for him; he had almost hugged her. He did however wish her well and when he patted her arm, was alarmed at how Mrs Hennessey jumped and seemed to be in pain.

It had been worth the extra money despite the mops being so shoddy he would not be able to give them away. He must be going soft, he thought, but at least the kids might get a treat. No-one had much but those two tots seemed to have very little of anything and he had never known children as quiet in their own home. As he pushed these thoughts from his mind, he sighed heavily and drove away.

Abigail stared at the extra two shillings before dropping the coins into the pocket of her apron. They say good things come in threes and today had brought two wonderful events. She hoped that the third one would be even better and as she waved at Mr Thompson's van until it was out of sight, she felt happier than she had done in months. When Charlie came in for his tea, she would give him the whole ten shillings and then at least she owed him nothing and had a bit extra to spend. The first wonderful event was that they had been given a date to move to a new area and every spare penny would be needed for the new house they had been allocated now that the transfer was finalised. Two more weeks and it would be a fresh start for all of them. Abigail hugged herself and simultaneously winced in pain as she touched the bruise that was still lingering on her arm even though it was weeks old. She quickly replaced the grimace with a smile as her neighbour shouted to her.

"Here Abigail, can you use up this apple pie? I made far too much and my lot won't eat it all. Here you go, enjoy that after your tea". Abigail gratefully took the large pie that had been cooked on a dinner plate and felt her mouth begin to water as the aroma of warm apple rose when she lifted the tea towel that was covering the sweet treat.

As the two women stood and chatted, Abigail realised her third good thing of the day had just happened and smiled gratefully at the woman next door. At least the children would go to bed with tummies that were not quite as empty tonight and Charlie would be delighted
with the home-made pie. He might even give her a compliment but even a kind word would do.

****

The tea chests stood in the hallway of the house in Mill Dam Lane and each one was full to the brim with items from each room. Everything had to be wrapped in newspaper and there had to be no gaps as each item was packed. Charlie insisted on lifting each chest and wriggling it to make sure nothing moved and that way, nothing would get broken.

Abigail had never been happier and as she cleaned each empty room ready for the next police family to use. She was singing along to Frank Sinatra's song, Strangers in The Night, as it echoed around the empty space from the wireless despite the volume being on a low setting. Charlie had been so kind to her for two whole weeks now and Abigail hoped that the move would be an end to his bad tempers and that he might relax once the past was left firmly behind them all. They could be a normal family somewhere else, where no one knew that she couldn't have children and had to adopt. Hannah and John would have friends to play with as there were children the same ages living in the adjoining police house and her new neighbours had already invited her for a cuppa. Best of all, Charlie was going to be
miles away from that woman and even though he said he had completely broken ties with her, Abigail could not fully believe it. This fresh start would do every one of her family the power of good.

As the last of the furniture was loaded into the removal van, Abigail checked each room to make sure that nothing had been left behind. She wanted no trace of her ever having lived in this house to be found. In fact, Abigail would be more than happy never to set foot in this town again as it had brought her nothing but trouble in her private life and publicly was not much better. The gossips had seen to it that she was not accepted and she was sick and tired of being treated so rudely by strangers. Never having to return was high on the list of things Abigail wanted to happen in her new life.

Chapter 10.

The house was on Edge Lane in a town in Liverpool called Thornton. It was much bigger than the house they had just moved from. Abigail felt at home the moment she had walked in. It was a warm house that somehow felt right, somehow peaceful and quiet despite being on a main road.

The Hennesseys had been here for six months now and life was good. Abigail had made friends with the neighbours, well, with the ladies who lived either side of her and was often popping in to one house or another for a chat and a cuppa. They didn't seem to mind when she called and welcomed her with open arms. They were happy to tell her all about the town, the best places to shop, the bus routes into the city and a hundred and one other things. They didn't mind if they called to see if the family had settled in over the first few months, but were turned away when Charlie was around.

Both neighbours thought it was strange that they were not invited in, because Abigail's husband seemed to be so pleasant and friendly and always spoke when he saw them anywhere. In fact, he sometimes seemed to be too friendly. Maybe it was just their imagination, but Charlie Hennessey always seemed to be flirting with each of the women
when he saw them alone but they couldn't be sure. They had discussed how they were made to feel by him if they bumped into him on the street and had both agreed that they felt uncomfortable but were not sure why. They put it down to the fact that he had strange coloured eyes – hazel eyes – and then promptly laughed the whole conversation away. They both thought it would be better to keep Abigail's husband at a distance but were not prepared to voice this. After all, Abigail was a lovely woman and they had come to enjoy her company even if it was only when he was at work or away at the weekends with the local fishing club at those

competitions that they had over two days. If Charlie didn't want her to have people in their house, then that was how it was, but both women found it to be very peculiar, especially as Abigail always had a reason to keep them out and was not always to be believed.

Abigail hated the fact that she had to lie to her friends but was grateful that they didn't ask questions. How on earth could she explain that everyone who came into the house had to be invited by Charlie personally and hell would freeze over before he let those two silly women, as he called them, into his house? No, Charlie did not want her socialising with these down to earth women with hearts of gold and Abigail knew why.

Charlie Hennessey felt as though the area he had been forced to move to was not much better than the area he had grown up in and he had gone backwards in his standing in the community after living in Burscough. The people were loud and laughed over the simplest of things that were not even funny to Charlie. Everyone who lived close by was too quick to want to befriend you and pass the time of day with you and this unsettled him. If he was to keep things to his exacting standards, then he had to keep people out of his house. Abigail, on the other hand, was feeling like she had lived here for years. She was exactly where she wanted to be forever and was thriving on her new way of life in this salt of the earth place on the outskirts of Liverpool, a place that reminded her so much of her life in the heart of Lancashire where people were kind and the community spirit was inclusive.

****

"I have to go," Charlie stated. "I can't let the team down and anyway we were only going to my mother's house. Let's face it, she really couldn't care less if she sees you or the kids ever again and it always upsets you that she is so different with them compared to her other grandchildren. You know how hard she has tried to like them but you have to accept the fact that she will never call them family. You are lucky that she tolerates them and still lets them into the house. She wouldn't if I hadn't threatened that she would not see me again if she did

keep you lot out. I think you need to be grateful the children still have some sort of grandma they can mention on my side. Look, I have fought your corner and I'll speak to my mam about being more accepting of the kids so can you just let me go to the competition without an argument. It's not as though you had made any firm plans to visit *your* aunty is it? Really Abigail, I don't know what all the fuss is about and like I said, I'll get a few days leave either side of my next weekend off and we can go to your brother's house."

Abigail knew she had been manipulated into submission yet again but the thought of a few days with her brother and his wife in Somerset, with good food and the children getting new clothes for the mini break was more than enough for her to smile at Charlie and to insist that he went to his fishing weekend as he was so kind and generous. Abigail scrambled out of bed quickly as the last thing she wanted was for any demands to be made on her to make love. Anyway, the children were awake and were shouting to get up.

"That's my girl!" grinned Charlie. "Now, go and fetch me a cuppa and the paper. It's just been delivered so I'll have half an hour lie in and a peaceful read before I get ready to go. Oh, and iron my good shirt once you've done that. The Captain is treating us to some supper in a posh hotel so I will have to look smart."

Abigail had sent John to bed. Hannah had been in bed for an hour and was fast asleep. Despite her best efforts to keep her son awake so that she had some company for a little while longer, he had fallen asleep on the chair so she shook him gently and helped him to his bed. Abigail had decided that she would give John time to settle into a deep sleep and telephone her mother.

That was another a good thing about this house. It was classed as a police station for Thornton as the nearest main station was a couple of miles away in Crosby and because of that, it had a party line telephone that was shared with the police house next door so that people of the town could call for help if the need arose. It also meant that Abigail could speak to her mother for fifteen minutes a week and that once her time was up, her mother could call her back to carry on the conversation. Abigail was looking forward to telling her mother that they would be coming to Somerset in a few weeks- time and to ask if she would let her brother know so that they could be ready for visitors.

The telephone was beeping. It took Abigail a while to figure out where the noise was coming from as it had never happened before and when she realised what it was, lifted the receiver and listened. "A call for you," said her neighbour. "I'll swap the line now."
Abigail stared at the phone in horror as the words sank in and she started shaking uncontrollably. She grabbed the tiny hall table to steady herself and put the receiver back into the cradle cutting off the angry voice and cruel words that she was hearing. Then slowly, she walked into the sitting room and sat heavily on the easy chair by the roaring coal fire. She was suddenly cold to the bone and as she tried to make sense of the one-sided conversation, the icy fingers of fear gripped her heart and made her gasp in disbelief.

****

Abigail had been unusually quiet when the children got up this morning and they had been frightened that she would

start to shout at them again. Their Mum had been really happy since they had moved to Thornton and it was ages since she had shouted at them. She hadn't told them they were naughty once or hit them really hard for ages. Today was different and so was their Mum but they didn't dare ask anything. John had spent most of the day in the garden aimlessly kicking a football around and Hannah had kept herself busy practicing her writing and reading her new library book. She had not uttered a word unless her mother had asked her something or told her to do a job or eat her dinner. The little girl who was now nearly seven, still worried about having her tongue cut out and knew that by being quiet she
would stop this happening. Hannah instinctively knew it was because her Dad was fishing again and hoped that when he got home, her Mum would go back to being happy and kind.

Abigail had tried desperately to keep herself happy so that the children wouldn't notice she was angry and upset, but when she had slipped on water that had been spilled on the linoleum in the kitchen, that was the final straw. When the children laughed heartily at her mishap, Abigail screamed at them to get out of her sight. Even though she knew how much she was scaring the children, Abigail was unable to stop herself. The children were rooted to the spot and when Abigail flew at them with her fist shaking, they both ran out of the kitchen and hid under the stairs until they felt brave enough to go their separate ways and find something to do. Ignoring her children, Abigail had systematically cleaned the whole house only stopping to make a sandwich for lunch and ordering the children to tidy away their toys before they could eat. Her head was pounding and she had no aspirin in the house. She was desperate to lie down as she was feeling sick but knew that she had to wait for Charlie to come home and as long as the children stayed quiet, she would manage somehow to keep her composure and the threatening migraine at bay.

The day had dragged on but at long last it was time to put the children to bed and all Abigail had to do was the ironing. Just hers and the children's clothes would be done. Then she could sit down and think about the best way to talk to Charlie.

She woke to find him standing over her, smiling happily and gently calling her name. Charlie Hennessey had had a really good weekend on his fishing trip and had won a trophy. He had also been saying a final goodbye to his lover from Burscough as he was determined to make a clean break from the past once and for all. His ladylove had accepted that it was finished and as they made love for the last time, they both held each other and cried when the act was completed.

His wife was happy living in Thornton and Charlie felt better when he came home to see her smiling and welcoming him with a kiss. She looked so much more relaxed and even the kids were behaving themselves. The house was always clean and tidy and Abigail had managed to get a cleaning job for three mornings a week so there was more money for him to spend on his drink, cigarettes and sports events. Life was looking up and she was becoming the wife he had to have. Her illness had not left her as bad as the doctors had said she would be and apart from the odd migraine, Charlie had convinced himself his wife was totally normal in the head department. Anyway, if Charlie wanted a bit on the side, he had a much
bigger area to choose from. Maybe living on the outskirts of a city had its plusses and he had the added bonus of stealing away for secret meetings by using the fishing club as his cover whenever he wanted.

Abigail smiled at Charlie when she realised that she was sitting in the armchair. She couldn't remember what time she had fallen asleep and had no idea what time it was now. In fact, she couldn't really understand where she was. Charlie began to tell her about the fishing competition, how the fish he caught had made the whole team overall winners and how much praise he had got from the others, as Abigail began to come back from the void that had momentarily left her without any memory.

As her recall grew, every word of the terrible telephone call began to run through her head and before she could control her thoughts, the words came out. Her voice was low and she knew that her speech was slow. Each word seemed to be forced out deliberately without any emotion or change of pitch. It was almost as though someone else was speaking because Abigail did not recognise her own voice.

Charlie, on the other hand, had moved away from his wife and sat heavily on the settee. He was so shocked by his wife's words, that he felt as though he as going to pass out. There
was nothing he could say to her. He had been caught, well and truly caught. "I'm going to bed," he muttered. "Let's talk in the morning once the kids are at school."

Abigail stood and poured more coal onto the glowing embers that signified the fire was dying. Then she lay down on the settee and waited for the flames to flicker into life, hoping the coming warmth would melt the ice-cold atmosphere left by her husband as he shut the door.

Chapter 11

Abigail was crying. She was trying desperately to stop her breath catching at the back of her throat. When this happened, she was unable to talk and a strange strangled sound was all that she could make. It meant that Charlie was able to talk freely and to justify his actions once again and Abigail did not want this to happen. This time, Abigail thought, she would not back down and forgive him or accept his explanations that he was convinced she would believe. Abigail blew her nose loudly so that she cleared her airways and could talk once again.

"You told me it was over Charlie and I was stupid enough to believe you. It would have been so much easier for everyone if you had just gone to be with her and left us behind. I have had my doubts about it really being finished for a while now and kept telling myself it was my imagination. But guess what Charlie, I was right all along. Do you know what a relief that is? No, you will never know because you don't care. You don't care about anyone but yourself, your standing in the community, your needs. Always about you Charlie Hennessey and how you can wriggle out of all the mess you cause. Well, what are you going to come up with next? How are you going to make it *my* fault once again? I'm waiting for your answer Charlie."

He sighed and looked intently into his wife's eyes. Surely, she could see how distressed he was. He hadn't slept a wink. How was he meant to sleep when Abigail was crying downstairs, when he could hear her sobs even with the pillow over his head? He couldn't go to her and comfort her. Charlie Hennessey did not know how to comfort anyone. Not properly, not as a husband should be able to do when the woman he had married was hurting. Not when he was the cause of her hurt and was, for the first time since being a boy, scared of the repercussions of his actions.

"Abigail, it won't matter what I say. All I can do is hope that you will forgive me. I know I'm asking a lot and if I lose you and the children because of what I did, I have only got myself to blame. If I could turn the clock back, believe me, I would but we both know that's never going to happen. Look, I'll take you to her house and she can tell you what happened. We can go now. Honestly, it's finished. I told her I had to make our marriage work and that it was the last time we would ever be together. It wasn't part of the plan to end up, well, in bed, but it just happened".

As she tore her eyes from his, Abigail began to wonder if Charlie was actually telling her the truth. He had not shouted like he did when he was hiding something or blaming her. He looked genuinely upset and that was something Abigail had never seen in her husband.
Charlie Hennessey seemed to be different. Smaller and scared. Did she really want to ask that woman? No, but if he was being honest then he would take her. If he wasn't, then he would wriggle out of it.

She stood up and said, "I'll just get my coat and we can go. I don't care if my hair is a mess and I don't want any make up on. I want her to see what pain looks like. Come on Charlie, I want to go right now. I want to save my marriage. I took vows and I think I have just met the for worse bit head on so let's go and I can start working on the for better bit." Charlie nodded and went to get the keys for the car.

****

The car came to a stop outside a row of council houses. Drab grey paint and blue doors were the main feature of every house. A line of identical boxes with no character. In between two houses there was a passage that led to the back of the house and Abigail wondered how often Charlie had sneaked into this woman's home using this entry in the cover of darkness.

As much as she didn't want to look, Abigail watched as her husband walked up one of the paths and knocked on the door. When it opened, her eyes drank in every inch of the woman who stood on the step and Abigail felt as though her heart was about to stop beating.

The woman was everything Abigail wasn't. She was slim with blonde hair in a short symmetrical style, dressed in the latest fashion of block colours in a dress that was just above the knee and looking very neat and tidy. The mod style it was called, or so it said in the papers. All the young girls in Thornton were dressed like this and the young men wore thin-legged trousers and a long jacket with a jumper underneath when they went out dancing. Charlie said that fashion was nothing but a gateway to trouble as all those he locked up at the weekend dressed this way and he was right. Just look at this woman. Nothing but trouble.

Abigail felt like a frumpy old woman despite being only 33, but then, that's what having children did to you. Took every penny, took your time to look good, took your identity as an individual, took your self-esteem.

Suddenly, Abigail started to laugh, a sort of snigger that grew to a hysterical, uncontrolled nervous noise and she wound down the window and shouted: "Well, I thought she was going to be something special. Just look at the state of *her.* She might be the height of fashion but
there's no getting away from the fact that she's nothing but a trollop. Oh, Charlie, how stupid of me to think that I was so worried that you had found yourself a beautiful film star but you got yourself a right little tart instead!"

As her husband stood with his head held high, Abigail laughed even louder as the woman turned and fled into the house, slamming the door behind her. Charlie walked slowly towards the car, breathing deeply so that he could keep his emotions in check. Nine years to go. Not too long in the bigger scheme of things and as soon as that so-called daughter of his was fifteen, all you would see was a trail of dust as he got the hell out of this life he was trapped in and then he could do exactly what he wanted.

Chapter 12.

Abigail walked along Edge Lane with her head bowed. She was aware of people passing by but didn't want to have to acknowledge anyone at the moment. They might see that she was upset and to cope with a kindness was a step too far right now.

The church was only a few minutes' walk away and the sooner she got there the better she would feel. It was a strange shaped church known fondly as the "threepenny bit" and was unlike the older style of churches that Abigail had worshipped in.

It was a relatively new church and the foundation stone had been laid in 1959 by Archbishop Heenan and from this was built the octagonal building that represented a centralised altar. It didn't matter where you sat in this church you always had a good view of the altar and somehow the congregation felt more involved with the many different services that were held there. Despite it being modern, St William of York church was still a church and that's all that mattered to Abigail.

As Abigail walked to the door, she began to wonder if she was doing the right thing. Would the Priest be able to help her or would she leave feeling more wretched than she already did? "Please let me find a solution," she offered up to the statue of the Sacred Heart that was watching down on her from its elevated place on the wall outside and welcoming Abigail to enter the building.

Dipping her fingers into the small bowl of holy water, Abigail dutifully blessed herself and went to sit on one of the long pews closest to the altar. Genuflecting quickly, she shuffled to the middle of the pew and stared intently at the beautifully carved crucifix, willing God to give her answers as to how she could deal with the latest upset that was once again her husband's doing.

"Mrs Hennessey?"

A soft Irish voice interrupted Abigail's fervent praying and as she lifted her head, she found herself staring directly into the Priest's eyes that were full of concern for her. Abigail could feel the tears beginning to well and hurriedly searched for her handkerchief to wipe them away. This was not a time for tears and Abigail knew that if she was offered one ounce of pity, she would crumble completely and not be able to talk to this man of God. This had to be done with decorum and calmness as Abigail knew that she only had this one opportunity to speak of her unhappiness and she had to get it right.

Father Fletcher was quite shocked to see Abigail in such a state as it was only last week he had been in her home on a pastoral visit. Everything had been fine when he was there and the Priest had been delighted when he was invited to stay for tea with the family. Later, Mr Hennessey had got out the whiskey whilst this good woman got the children ready for bed and left the men to talk. Nothing seemed to be amiss in this household, so what on earth had happened to bring her to the Lord's house in such a state?

"He's been seeing another woman," Abigail said. "He nearly lost his job because of it and that's why we ended up in Thornton. Charlie said it was over and done with and I have tried so hard to forgive him but I don't think I can. Not now. He has completely ruined my life and made me feel so bad. I don't want to go on any more- living like this- and I need you to tell me what I can do to make it stop. Please, Father Fletcher, I need your help."

As the Priest listened, Abigail began to tell of the events that had led her to seek answers that she was hoping her God would reveal to her and although he was shocked to learn of a different Mr Hennessey to the man he knew, he was not sure how to advise this woman.

Divorce was out of the question and as Mr Hennessey was an atheist, Father Fletcher knew that to speak with this man would be a waste of breath. It always got complicated when one part of a married couple was of a different religious belief and Charlie Hennessey wasn't even a believer of any god. The only thing that he could offer Mrs Hennessey was to pray to the Lord for a way forward. As far as he was concerned, Mr Hennessey was just another in a long line of men who had had a fling with an unsuitable woman. It was the women who should know better; that was the way of the world for men and it was, after all a man's world.

As they prayed together, the Priest was astounded when Mrs Hennessey announced that she had got the answer she was looking for, thanked him for his help and promptly stood up and left the church. God worked in very mysterious ways and this was one of those times that Father Fletcher was so pleased that he no longer had to be involved with this mess. As he made the sign of the cross, he sighed with relief and headed to the vestry to check on the stocks of communion wine.

Abigail walked back to her house with her head held high and a look of determination on her face that had passers by staring at her in wonder.

Chapter 13.

Abigail pushed the swing higher as Hannah squealed in delight. She glanced at her daughter's happy face quickly before turning her gaze back onto the blue front door that was in the middle of the row of terraced houses. If she missed her chance it would be another month before she could get back and Abigail had to sort this today. The neighbour said the woman, who Abigail only knew as Pauline, had popped to the shops and shouldn't be too long.

"No, thank you, I'll just wait outside," Abigail told Pauline's neighbour. "I'll take the children to the park for a run around. Thanks for the offer, but we are fine." Smiling, Abigail gently took hold of Hannah's hand and led her down the path. John trailed behind his mother and once they had reached the park, he ran towards the slide, ignoring Abigail's demands to come and play with Hannah.

After what seemed like hours rather than the few minutes it actually was, Abigail saw the woman heading towards the row of houses and she hurriedly pulled Hannah from the swing and walked over to the slide to where John was sitting. He had climbed the steps and stayed
there. His expression one of total indifference as Abigail told him to stay with Hannah whilst she went to see a lady.

Hannah, however, began to bombard her mother with question after question and Abigail knew she had to somehow keep her daughter away from that house and not let her hear one word that was going to be spoken.

No. Hannah could not come with her.
No. Hannah had to stay with John.
No. Abigail would not tell her who the lady was.
No. John would not leave her and he would play nicely.

No. John would not hit her if he knew what was good for him.

As Hannah's face took on that mutinous look, Abigail resorted to the only thing she had left to get her wilful daughter to stay put.

"Move from here if you dare, Hannah Theresa Hennessey. If you follow me, I will slap your legs so hard that you won't be able to walk again. Now do as you are told and stay here. If you are good and do what I want, I might buy you some sweets but you have to stay here and not move from the slide."

Then Abigail turned from her children and walked quickly towards the road and that blue door behind which was the proof of Charlie Hennessey's wrongdoing, ignoring her daughter's pleas for her to come back even though the child said she was scared…

The door opened and Pauline's eyes went wide with shock. She knew who this woman was and had never imagined that Abigail would ever come calling. Charlie had promised her that his wife would never come here again. Well, that was just one more lie to add to the list of that bloody sweet talker Charlie Hennessey. Pauline wasn't sure what to say but knew that whatever was to be said was not going to be voiced on the street and curtly said, "You'd better come in."

"Is he here?" Abigail asked. When Pauline shook her head, she stepped into the hallway, glanced back at the park to make sure Hannah was still by the slide and followed this woman into the parlour. "I half expected him to be here but then again… can you leave the door open so I can keep an eye on the children?"

Pauline smiled at Abigail and invited her to sit down. When both women had sat down, Pauline began to talk and after a while, Abigail began to feel some sort of affinity for this young woman.

"I need you to know that the last time I saw him in any sort of relationship way was on that fishing trip. That's when I fell pregnant, that weekend. I wish with all my heart that I hadn't agreed to meet him. Yes, I loved him, well, I thought I did. I really only loved the danger and now look at what it's led to. He was like a drug that I needed to have over and over again in order to feel alive but now I can see it was all about him. He somehow brainwashed me into believing everything he said and I accepted it all. I trusted him and now I've been left well and truly holding the baby, well for now…"

As Pauline's voice wavered, Abigail stood and went to look in the pram where her husband's child lay sleeping. The boy didn't look like Charlie but there was a slight resemblance to Charlie's youngest sister. Abigail moved back quickly, not wanting the child to see her as he suddenly squirmed and began to awaken.

"He knows I'm here," Abigail said. "I thought he would have been the one to open the door but anyway I'm glad he has somehow spoken to you about the boy".

Pauline looked confused and suddenly Abigail realised that Charlie had not spoken to Pauline about his son and making the infant part of her family. Horrified that her husband could be so cruel to both her and this young woman, Abigail suddenly felt as though she was going to pass out and sat down heavily on the chair.

"You don't know, do you? I'm here to ask if you will let me have the baby. Charlie wants his son in his life and if you hand him over, I will raise him with the other two. He said he was going to come and talk to you. Easier all round, Charlie said. Oh, and at least you can get on with your life and start again. You are only young".

Pauline ran to the pram and lifted her son, instinctively protecting her baby.

"Charlie contacted me and told me to get the boy registered but not to put him as the father on the birth certificate and I did what he wanted. I agreed to not putting his name on as Charlie said he would lose his job but wanted to help with the costs of raising him so it was better all round. I believed he wanted to be a part of his son's life in some small way. He said he would sort out money every month and he would be classed as a distant relative. He said he had to stay with you and your two children and the only way he could support us was by being married to you. Charlie told me he had discussed it with you and that you had agreed. He said you wouldn't tolerate his true child as part of your family and he had to consider everyone. Now I can see he's only considered himself."

Pauline was sobbing loudly as she said, "He's never given me a penny and he won't speak to me. I have written letter after letter and phoned the police station and all he says is that I have no claim on him as the baby is not registered in his name. My family have disowned me and I can't manage. I'm in a right mess but am determined to keep *my* son and you and your husband can go to hell."

Abigail went to the woman and gently put her arms around both Pauline and the baby, soothing them both until a familiar voice made her jump back.

"Mummy, I need a wee," Hannah said.

****

They were sitting in the café next to the bus station in Ormskirk and had just made it in time before it closed. Half an hour, the woman behind the counter said before she shut for
the day. Plenty of time for a drink and a warm, she said kindly to the woman who looked upset.

The café owner was sure she had seen the girl before. She didn't recognise the boy and that was what made her wonder if she was right. She never forgot any child that she had seen. After all, they brought in the parents and that meant more money.

It was something about the way the little girl looked as she wriggled constantly on her seat watching the bubbles rise to the top of the bottle of pop, as she moved the straw up and down causing the gasses to expand and fizz but taking great care to stop before the foaming growth spilled over onto the table.

It was the serious face that suddenly lit up with joy as she told her mother to watch what she could do. That smile that made the child's eyes glow with pride. Familiar, but where from?

"Hannah, drink that properly and stop playing about.
You're going to make a mess," Abigail warned her daughter.
"Now drink up, the bus is due to leave in ten minutes and we can't get back home if we miss it."

Hannah sucked hard on the straw and swallowed noisily which led her into a fit of giggles as she looked at her mother's angry face. Her Mummy didn't shout at her when they were outside and Hannah felt safe enough to push her luck. As the little girl looked straight at Abigail, she did it again, hoping to make her Mummy less sad and maybe laugh too. Mummy had wanted this other baby and Hannah liked the idea of a little brother.

Suddenly Hannah felt a stinging pain on her hand that made her drop the bottle and let out a shriek that was caused more by shock than pain.

The café owner was making her way over to the table with a cloth to mop up the mess when she heard the woman admonish the child and realised where she had seen the child before.

"Hannah Theresa Hennessey, I am sick to death of you not doing what you are told. Now get your coat on and wait outside for me. Look at the mess you've made. You're worse than a baby," Abigail hissed none too quietly.

As Hannah stood, she stared at her mother. "Well when we get that new baby from the lady by the park at least I won't be the one always in trouble. It will be the baby and I will be glad".

Abigail prayed silently that the woman with the cloth hadn't heard too much and hurriedly told John it was time to leave. How on earth was she to convince Hannah not to talk of this outing again? If she made it into a big deal, Hannah would never stop mentioning it and this was a secret that had to be buried, not just confined to the cupboard like the other skeletons that lurked and rattled around in her life.

It was the surname that registered first with the apron-clad woman. Hennessey. That Charlie, the policeman from Burscough who suddenly moved to Liverpool, thought the café owner. An affair with a young woman who ended up pregnant was the gossip doing the rounds on that one and that was exactly what the café owner needed everyone to think.

After all, she and Charlie had only seen each other a few times and when she bumped into him at the corner shop with the girl, he had introduced the child as his daughter, Hannah. The girl had eyed her seriously and then smiled beautifully when Charlie introduced her as his special friend. She ended the fling there and then as she didn't want to be the cause of two lots of children being hurt.

Well, she had seen him once more, about four months ago for old times' sake. He'd been passing by after wrapping up a case he had been involved in before he moved away and had persuaded her to kiss him goodbye forever. He said he loved her and like a fool, she fell for his charms.

Rumours had started in Ormskirk about her and the policeman but had been quickly dealt with because of the break in at the café. That was where it started. He comforted her with a hug and one thing led to another. The Police had to call to keep her updated on what was happening and so what if it was always PC Hennessey? He had been assigned to look after this case and was doing so in more ways than one. Thankfully, her husband was delighted that they were expecting their fourth child and had no idea it was not his.

The young woman in Burscough had taken all the attention off any of that rotten policeman's other infidelities, when the pregnancy was too far gone to hide and the gossips helped her, the respectable café owner, to stay under the radar. They couldn't prove a thing and soon she was off the hook once Pauline got their full attention over her scandalous behaviour.

The café owner felt sorry for this woman, this Mrs Hennessey and as she wiped the table, smiled kindly. "No harm done, love, there's worse problems in the world than a bit of spilt pop. There we are, all cleaned away and forgotten about. You look after those two children of yours and have a safe journey back to Liverpool. Now I don't mean to rush you, but I'm closing in a minute." As she wiped the table, the vigorous movement hid the shaking of her hand.

Abigail left the café and wondered how on earth the woman knew she was going to Liverpool. Nothing had been mentioned as far as she could remember and Abigail was sure she had never clapped eyes on the woman before.

"'Bye Lady," Hannah shouted as Abigail opened the door and pushed John hurriedly onto the street.

"That's Daddy's special friend," Hannah importantly told her mother.

Abigail turned to look at the woman who ran the café and her blood ran cold as she realised that beneath the apron was the unmistakable swell of a belly that held a life. The café owner was holding her stomach and this accentuated the early roundness that would soon be visible to all.

Abigail dragged the children to the bus station and almost threw them onto the bus that was waiting to leave. She remembered Charlie had told her of the café in Ormskirk that had been burgled and he had had to do an extra patrol back in his old patch in case it happened again and they caught the thieves.

It was the only night he had been home late and had muttered something about Ormskirk, looking sheepish and quickly getting changed out of his uniform. He put his shirt to soak in the sink saying he had spilled tea down it and didn't want it to stain. Abigail didn't question this although she thought Charlie being helpful was strange. It was the only night that he mentioned Ormskirk but everyone knew, it only took once to make a baby. Look at how she had come to get these two children to call her own. One moment of passion had a lot to answer for, for so many people in this world.

As she watched her children, Abigail wondered if "daddy's special friend" was the reason for that café owner's pregnancy and shuddered involuntarily.

"That's just nonsense" she silently chided herself and only just stopped herself from asking Hannah how she knew the lady. After all, Charlie probably had children the length and breadth of the country and to be honest, the less she knew the better.

All she had to do was find a way to forget about this fly blow of her husbands that lived in Burscough and somehow get her marriage and her children's future back on an even keel. If she kept telling herself it didn't matter, just like she had done many times before, she would survive and it wouldn't matter.

It was strange that somehow, Abigail couldn't live without Charlie even though she knew he treated her disgustingly. He had drained almost every drop of her identity and she needed him to tell her how to live. She wasn't sure when it had happened, she only knew that she had to find a way to get on with it.

As the children started to squabble over something and nothing, Abigail closed her eyes and let them carry on. If she couldn't see what was happening, she wouldn't have to deal with it and she had no energy left to deal with another thing. Anyway, there was no-one else on the upstairs deck of the bus apart from them so as with so many other events that had happened, Abigail told herself again that t didn't matter.

Chapter 14.

Abigail had to have a job. Her cleaning job for an elderly spinster had come to an end the day the lady had died. The spinster's solicitor had informed her that she was no longer required and that was that. She needed extra cash and had been up and down The Crescent asking if they needed staff in the shops that served the town but was always told not at the moment.

They all had her name and telephone number in case anything came up but Abigail knew that the chances of getting any work was slim. Everyone who worked in the shops was either related to the owners or had been there for years and were happy to work for good employers. There was no way anyone would leave unless it was absolutely necessary and there was always someone else to be taken on before her.

It was a well-used shopping area and boasted a launderette, two small food stores, newsagents, post office and a chandler amongst others. There was a butcher shop and a fruit and vegetable shop and Abigail often went in to the greengrocers to buy the bruised fruit, mainly apples, that were sold for a penny. This was when things got desperate and it meant the children had some vitamins that would help to keep them healthy. The butchers sold
scrag end cheaply too so at least there was a bit of meat that she could mince and make a good meal of cottage pie that was filling and not too fatty if you got it when it was piping hot. Charlie had to have different food. Better quality as he wouldn't eat muck, as he called it and that meant she was always looking for money saving ways to keep herself and the children from being too hungry.

It was a godsend when Charlie agreed to pay for the children's school dinners as it meant that at least they got one good meal a day and a pudding too. Hannah was a server and often told Abigail how she liked it when someone at her table was off school as she got more food and was too full for tea.

Although it broke Abigail's heart that she couldn't feed her children properly all the time, she was always grateful to know that her daughter was not starving and that the less she could spend any day on a meal would subsidise food at the weekend, even if it was extra mashed potato. It also meant that John could have a bigger portion as he was growing so fast and had developed hollow legs, as she often joked with him. He was constantly looking for more and more food now that he was changing from a boy to a young man.

Money was still a major issue with her and Charlie and Abigail knew it was pointless to ask him for more. He always had enough for his cigarettes daily, a few pints at night – every night if truth be told and his special treats such as a piece of steak or a fillet of fresh salmon that he ate when the children were in bed. If he was feeling generous, Abigail sometimes got a tiny share.

Charlie still went away for the odd weekend too and had so many clothes to choose from when he was off duty whilst she had to make do with one dress all week that was protected with a pinny and a dress for Sunday Best as you always had to look smart in church or if she had to go and see Charlie's family in Accrington.

The children didn't fare any better than her where clothes were concerned but at least Charlie would buy shoes as their little feet grew and sometimes rigged them out when everything they had was too small or only fit to be turned into rags. It was always the cheapest of clothing and Charlie refused to let the children have any of the fashionable clothes that were becoming available. They cost too much money, he said.

Abigail was an expert at making knickers for Hannah out of any salvageable bits of material as the child only ever had one decent pair for school that were washed out as required. Usually on a Friday night so they were ready for Monday morning and the rest of the week. If Hannah stained them, they were rinsed in the old water from the washing up bowl after all the dishes had been done and placed inside her daughter's pillowcase as the heat from Hannah's head was enough to dry them so she could wear them the next day.

Weekends meant Hannah had to wear whatever was available or sometimes wore a pair of old tight tops of her mother's that had part of the legs cut off to hide her modesty. Abigail used to make it into a game so that Hannah would just do as she was asked and wear the dreadful items. Abigail had convinced her daughter that it was what all little girls did so that they were used to wearing nylon when they were grown up.

There were many grown up days played between mother and daughter and Abigail sometimes let Hannah put on a touch of pink lipstick to make the game more realistic. Abigail hid her sorrow behind a bright smile as Hannah strutted around and they laughed together at the child's antics as she tried to apply the lipstick.

****

Abigail eventually got a job. It didn't bring in a great deal of money but at least it was something each week that was put towards the food bill and the children were better fed than
they had been in a long time. She had struck lucky as she had overheard a conversation about a job at the preparatory

school in Crosby as she waited for the bus to take her to the city.

The two women were discussing at length how an acquaintance had been treated so unfairly and dismissed on the spot for taking leftover food from the school kitchen. All because she hadn't asked and if you didn't ask, then you couldn't take. They said she had been stealing but at the end of the day, the women mused, it was going in the bin so what was the harm? Funny old world, they agreed as they waited to board the bus that was going to the city centre.

Abigail followed the two women onto the bus and sat down just behind them, hoping for more information on this school as the friends continued the conversation about the unfortunate woman sacked for taking a bit of cheese pie. It wasn't like the children of the school were being denied the food, one commented, as this school was the posh one in Crosby and who in their right minds would actually pay to send a young'un to school when you could send them for free? A bit different when they got older, but not when they were just out of nappies and knew nothing. Oh, and not named after a saint, the other added. What sort of a name was Childown House for any school? It sounded like some sort of home for waifs and strays, you know, like Nazareth House that took in orphans and the like. Actually, it was really Blundellsands the women agreed and promptly turned the conversation to clothing they hoped to get cheaply in St John's market.

The next stop was looming and Abigail quickly stood and made her way to the front of the bus. The conductor shouted, "Oi Missus, you haven't paid!" but Abigail ignored him and as the bus stopped, jumped down the steps and began to run as fast as she could. Charlie was on late shift and he would be able to take her in the car to the school. She needed to sort her hair, put on her good clothes and a bit of makeup would be needed and the sooner she got home, the sooner she could get to the school and ask for a job. Childown House would soon be looking at their new kitchen worker if she and Charlie had anything to do with it.

****

It was posh, Abigail thought, just like the two women on the bus had said. It was a huge house standing in its own grounds and Abigail felt slightly intimidated by the splendour that faced her. She looked at her husband and felt a shiver run down her spine. This area was just like the place that they got Hannah from over nine years ago and Abigail was sure that they were close to the dreadful hostel that she still thought of now and again. The house was different but it was the wide roads and well-maintained gardens that made Abigail wonder if
she was going to be working close to her daughter's first home. Whatever would she do if she was right and there was any talk about that place? They were rich topics of conversation, those hostels, and Abigail couldn't bear the thought of having to deny her daughter's start in life, but she couldn't really talk about it either as her well-kept secret of not being able to have children would come out.

Abigail decided that she would plead ignorance if any of this did happen and forced the unwelcome thoughts to the back of her mind. Ah, well, no going back now, she thought as Charlie guided her up the wide pathway to the front door.

Charlie had been delighted with her news about a job being available and had gone to great lengths to help her. He had found the telephone number of the school and spoke personally to someone about the "open position" as he called it. This had made Abigail smile as she heard Charlie Hennessey trying to sound like a cut above, to give a better impression of his standing than was necessary as, after all, it was a job in a school kitchen, not The Adelphi in Liverpool, but his manner had paid dividends and she had been offered a week's trial, starting tomorrow. Today, they wanted to meet her and show her round and, "Yes, of course PC Hennessey, it would be wonderful, a privilege in fact, if you were to be included in the tour," gushed the cook.

Abigail had been working in the school kitchens for two months. It was an easy job as most of the time she was washing the never-ending pile of pots, pans and trays that were generated as the cook made the food for the day.

It was good, wholesome food and there was always plenty for the school children and teachers to eat. Abigail was not allowed to help with the actual cooking but had been asked to prepare vegetables and peel endless potatoes whenever someone was off poorly. However, she was allowed to serve the children with their food and liked to help the tiny ones to sit properly and show them how to cut up meat and eat politely, just like John and Hannah had been taught.

The others who she worked with had accepted her and Abigail enjoyed her four hours of daily work with her dinner thrown in, Monday to Friday. There was usually extra food and if there was plenty, everyone got to take some home. If there was only a small amount, you had a set day to be offered the leftovers by cook and it had been pointed out to Abigail that if she took as much as a pea without permission, she would be dismissed on the spot. This made everyone laugh as one of the workers quipped, "Thought we could go to the bog whenever we wanted. Do we have to put our hands up too, like the kids in the classrooms Miss?"

But despite the joking, all the staff knew that cook was deadly serious and if you got sacked for pinching then the school made it really hard for you to get another job and it had been rumoured that one poor woman had been arrested for taking home some left over beef. It was also rumoured that when the police called at the woman's home, she had offered them a dish of meaty broth, which they had accepted and eaten before taking her away for questioning. They had to let her go when someone realised that the two officers had been handling stolen goods and inadvertently destroyed all the evidence.

****

Charlie was also being much kinder and more generous to Abigail now she had a job in such a place of standing. He had been out and bought her dresses, new shoes and a warm winter coat so that she fitted into her new surroundings and he didn't want Abigail to pay him back for the new items. He also paid for her to have her hair set every Friday in the ladies' salon that was near the police station in Crosby Village. He took her home in the police car so that the wind didn't damage her pretty curls and that meant she got a few days longer out of the style as long as she looked after it.

Abigail had finally done something that pleased Charlie Hennessey and she was so happy to think that at last, life was looking up since she had overheard the two women at a bus stop. If this was the best it could get, then Abigail Hennessey had no complaints whatsoever.

Charlie had even stopped going out as much and he was so amorous these days that Abigail knew her marriage was back on an even keel and there were no nasty surprises lurking. She knew to refuse Charlie anything in the bedroom would be giving him a reason to stray so despite her own wishes, just got on with it. He had stopped shouting at her too and he had not lifted his hand in temper for weeks. Best of all, he had booked them a proper holiday in a caravan in Scotland and was so proud of himself that he had taken her to the Nags Head for a celebratory drink and to tell anyone who would listen how wonderful it was to be a middle class man who was definitely going places.

Chapter 15.

Abigail was walking along College Road in Crosby. It was the start of the summer holidays and she had been asked to go into work to deep clean the kitchen at Childown House and to help with cleaning the classrooms too. It was full days for the next three weeks and Abigail had jumped at the chance. She would have extra money for their caravan holiday in Scotland and would be able to treat the children to ice cream every day or maybe buy a souvenir so they would always have a reminder of their first real holiday as a family. Two whole weeks of living by the beach in a box on wheels. Charlie said there was no toilet in it but there was a wash house which had shared toilets and spaces to wash. There was not much to do but if the weather was good, the beach was more than enough to keep the children happy. Abigail didn't care. It was the thought of a proper holiday that mattered, not where they went.

Hannah was allowed to go work with Abigail when the school was closed for the summer as all the children who were boarding there were returned to their parents. As her daughter chattered excitedly about the school, the caravan and a hundred and one other things, Abigail grunted now and then so her daughter would think she was listening whilst walking quicker and quicker until Hannah was actually trotting to keep up.

Abigail had to get to the post office to cash the family allowance that was due so that she could then get back home on the bus. She'd only just scraped up the fare for her and Hannah today for a one-way ticket but at least tomorrow it would be cheaper as she could get returns. Also, if they hurried, she might beat the queue and would get to work on time. It wouldn't look good to be late in front of her daughter and cook would have plenty to say on the matter. Cook was a stickler for time being kept and prided herself that the meals went out on time in the school every day.

As the post office came into sight, Abigail breathed a sigh of relief. There were only two people waiting for the door to open, which meant she would be able to slow her pace and still get to work on time. Hannah had started to whinge about how fast they were walking so Abigail slowed down and Hannah was once again able to keep up. They were nearly there when Abigail noticed a group of women coming from the opposite direction and they stopped right by the post office.

Strange, thought Abigail, all these women turning up at once. Maybe there would be two cashiers on the counter seeing though there were so many people to deal with and they would still get to the school on time. Better speed up in case any more people decide to join the queue. As Abigail grabbed for Hannah's hand and pulled her daughter along, the child
tripped and fell hard onto her knees. Hannah squealed in pain and as her mother hauled her to her feet and carried on her frantic pace, Hannah screamed as loudly as she could when she saw the blood running down her legs from the scrapes that the pavement had made.

The women in the queue all turned to see where the distraught sound of a child was coming from and Abigail stopped dead in her tracks. The majority of the women were heavily pregnant and this made them all stick out like a sore thumb but what really brought Abigail to a sudden stop was the fact that she was staring directly at that woman, the Matron who ran Berkley House mother and baby hostel.

"Don't leave my side or let go of my hand and do not stare at those ladies outside the post office," Abigail quietly told Hannah as she bent to look at her daughter's knees, wiping the blood away with a handkerchief. "They have all got big tummies as they are having babies and it's rude to stare. Now I want you to do exactly as I have told you and if anyone speaks to you, do not answer them," she continued.

Hannah's watery eyes met her mothers and Abigail realised all she had done was pique her daughter's insatiable appetite for information. The child's eyes widened and she asked, "Why are there so many? Are they all friends? Why do some not have big tummies and
Mummy, why do they all look so sad? Those ladies without a baby in their tummy, I mean and where are their babies as you said they all have big tummies and they haven't so what happened to their baby?"

Abigail sighed. "Hannah, just stay quiet please. Just stay by my side like I have said and be a good girl. Now, if you do as I want, I'll get you some plasters to put on your sore knees. You like plasters, don't you? But I will only get them if you do as you are told."

The door to the post office had opened and the people waiting on the street filed in leaving only one person outside and Abigail knew that she had been recognised by the Matron. "Please let me be wrong," Abigail muttered. "Please let it be anyone but her. Please don't let her speak to me."

Hannah winced as her mother tightened her grip on the tiny hand but knew if she made a fuss there would be no plasters even though the ladies with babies in their tummies were not there to stare at. Hannah felt so sad that she cried silently as they made their way across the road and headed towards the post office. "Where are the babies and why are they not with their mummies?" she wailed at the very moment they were passing the woman Abigail had never hoped to see again. "I need to know that the babies are…"
"Well, are you not going to answer the brat Mrs Hennessey?" a slurred voice asked. "Why don't you tell her why these little bastards are not with their mummies? Why

don't you tell her that these babies are so horrible that they have to go to new mummies? That their mummies are worthless sinners and that Theresa's real mummy hated her and was glad to be rid of her. Oh, I remember you and your husband Mrs Hennessey. I always said I would see my day with the both of you. The trouble you caused me the day you got that brat was something I will never forget and today's the day I get my own back".

The Matron's voice got louder until she was screaming the last few words and then she began to laugh hysterically, her alcohol fumed breath filling the air, making Abigail gag.

Then it seemed to Abigail that hell had broken loose. An arm flew past Abigail and there was a sickening crunch as a fist connected with the Matron's face. There were arms around Abigail's waist and she was being dragged away. Hannah had been lifted by a woman and was being taken out of harm's way. There was a mixture of raised voices, all female, all different accents berating the Matron in the background. Abigail was being roughly pushed and pulled towards her hysterical child until finally mother and daughter were clinging to each other and strange voices were trying to soothe and calm the child. The Matron was
lying on the pavement and as the sound of a police siren and a solitary blue flashing light came into view, the women surrounding her stepped back and fell silent.

****

Abigail didn't return to her job in the school kitchen. The cook was adamant. It wasn't anything personal but the reputation of the school was more important than one person.

If it had not been in the newspaper, The Crosby Herald, then they might have been able to keep her on. Luckily it had not got into the national newspapers as a few of the influential parents of the children had pulled strings.

The full weight of the Liverpool Catholic Children's Society had been used to protect their interest regarding the mother and baby hostel on Serpentine South. It had been an event that no-one wanted to be a part of as illegitimate children were unacceptable and had to be hidden from society as they were different. Damage limitation was needed and as it had only been in a small newspaper, then this would be easy to brush under the carpet.

It was the fact that the Church had been involved in the newspaper report that had been the deciding factor in the school letting Abigail go. To be linked to such a dreadful place that was full of sinners in the affluent area was not good for anyone and no matter how much cook felt heart sorry for this kind woman, there was no denying it, Mrs Hennessey was linked because of her adopted daughter.

They would give her a good reference and had paid her extra in her last pay packet. It was a thank you gift and for being so understanding that the good name of this wealthy establishment must not be blemished and to protect the children who attended here the cook stated. Cook wished her well and asked Abigail to use the back way out of the grounds as she handed over the buff coloured packet and bid Abigail goodbye.

Chapter 16.

The holiday was the perfect distraction. The Hennesseys had travelled to a small fishing village called Hopeman on the Moray Firth in Scotland. It was peaceful and the caravan was so close to the beach that you could hear the ebb and flow of the sea as you fell asleep and woke in the morning. Abigail had let the stress of daily life slide away and felt like she had a new lease of life as she breathed in the fresh air and walked along the clean, sandy shoreline.
She was feeling much better with each day that passed in this idyllic place and wished it could go on forever.

After the ordeal at the post office, all the upset had left her unable to concentrate and she had become very sleepy. She was forgetful too. She couldn't remember who Hannah was when her daughter had suddenly woken her one afternoon after she had nodded off in the chair when she had sat down to eat her dinner. Hannah had been terrified that her mother did not recognise her as she excitedly ran in from Brownies to show off the certificate that she had been awarded for being a good learner. Her mother had told Hannah to go back to her own house and family and no matter how hard Hannah tried to get her mother to acknowledge her, Abigail had no idea who this strange child was in her home and forced her daughter to go outside.
Abigail had eventually remembered her daughter and tried to make light of the situation, saying it was a joke but Hannah knew it was no laughing matter as it kept happening after Abigail had fell asleep. Hannah's mother had literally no recollection of who she was, who her child was and at times, thought she was living in her childhood home of Accrington. It only happened if she was suddenly roused from sleep and eventually Hannah learned not to waken her mother but to sit quietly until Abigail came to her senses and spoke to her daughter by name. Sometimes Hannah sat

silently for hours until her Dad came in for tea because yet again her Mum had slept the afternoon away.

Abigail had told Hannah not to mention this strange situation to anyone when Hannah asked why her Mum could not remember her. The girl could only hope that her Dad would not be recognised one day and take her Mum for some help. Her Mum said it didn't happen but Hannah knew it did. If she told her Dad, her Mum would be mad and Hannah might get sent away for good. Abigail had forcibly pushed her daughter out of the house twice now and found Hannah huddled in the outhouse crying quietly. She had laughed at Hannah when the child begged her mother not to send her away again as Abigail genuinely though Hannah was making up a story and being silly.

Somehow, Abigail always remembered Charlie when he came home and greeted him warmly. "Hello love," she would say when he woke her up. "What time is it?"

Abigail always called her husband "love", and Hannah didn't realise her Mum greeted all grow- ups, even strangers, in this way so Hannah thought it was about her only and that her Mum didn't want her any more, just like her real Mum didn't.

It was only since all that trouble outside the post office that Hannah had convinced herself her mother was going to send her away and it was compounded by the fact Abigail refused to talk of anything that happened to her daughter. Abigail said it didn't matter, but it mattered a great deal to the girl as she was scared.

****

Abigail found it strange that whilst they were on holiday, everything was easy to remember and she hoped that when they got back to Thornton, her memory would be better. It had been a bit of a struggle lately and she had had to write lists of what needed doing in the house each day. Charlie was getting angry again as the house was never tidy and most nights

there was no tea waiting for him. Abigail couldn't explain to her husband why her standards had slipped. She just couldn't remember why.

Chapter 17.

It was September and the start of a new school year. The children had been back for two weeks now and Abigail was enjoying the peace of the house all to herself. Her problems with her memory seemed to have been cured since the holiday and she was pleased that she no longer had to rely on as many lists and had got back into a good routine with housework.

Charlie had been wonderful too and had surprised her with a new upright vacuum cleaner, complete with spare bags to help her manage a bit better and get through the housework quicker.

Her delight was short-lived when Charlie said that it would be a godsend as now that Hannah was nearly eleven and was old enough to look after herself after school, Abigail had to get a full-time job. He had given her long enough to be out of a job and told her in no uncertain terms she had to be in work by November as it was her turn to buy the Christmas presents for the children. If she didn't work then they would get nothing.

Charlie hated Christmas and never wanted to celebrate it anyway. He worked every Christmas holiday so he could have New Year off and ended up in bed for at least a full dayonce he had been to every party he could find to gate-crash and had drunk himself into a stupor.

Abigail had thanked him for the vacuum cleaner and said she would start to look for a job once the children had gone to school. There was no point in upsetting him and she had enough to cope with, with her son's behaviour. She had kept her concerns about John to herself as the less involvement Charlie had, the better. It was probably something and nothing and Charlie only needed to be told if it was a serious matter.

Her husband was far too strict with John and took every opportunity to shout at him. Abigail worried about where it would end as John was getting old enough to have his own opinion and Charlie was hell bent on keeping the boy under his total control. It was so unfair on the boy but Abigail could not interfere. Her life was good at the moment and she was so much better at remembering if she kept Charlie happy and the thought of her husband turning nasty again was too much to contemplate. John would have to put up with his father until he could legally leave home.

****

John was at St. Bede's School. He had to get a bus there and back every day which was costing Abigail a fortune because she had forgotten to send the form to the council for the free travel pass. On top of that, she had had to find money for a school uniform as last year's school clothes were too small for him to wear. He was fourteen now and was long and thin with gangly arms and legs. He had always been quiet, but he was too quiet these days. Abigail was worried.

John had suddenly begun to demand money from Abigail for the school tuck shop even though he was taking his paper round money to buy something every day. He was also coming home so hungry that Abigail wondered if her son was actually eating anything. The money for school dinners was Charlie's responsibility and he gave John the ten pence he needed to hand into school every Friday morning for the following week's meals. No matter how hard Abigail tried, her son was adamant that he was fine and that school was fine too. When she had refused to give him any tuck shop money, John had stormed into the kitchen and Abigail gave him a minute to calm down before she followed him to explain that money was tight and tuck shop goods were a luxury not a necessity.

When the boy realised Abigail was in the kitchen, he slammed shut the drawer he had been looking in. As he did so, a ten pence piece fell from his hand and bounced across the
kitchen floor. John took one look at his mother and ran to the back door, yanked it open and ran as fast as he could away from the house.

****

"Charlie, please, Charlie just wait to hear the boy out. He's not a thief. There's something wrong at school but he won't tell me what it is." Abigail had stood between her husband and son who had come back into the house to apologise to his mother.

"I told him to take the money from my purse Charlie, please believe me love," she wheedled.

"Get out the bloody way woman or I'll knock you out of the way. There's no son of mine going to steal from anyone and as for you covering up for him, well, I always knew you were more for them two bloody kids than me, Abigail, but this time you can't make this into a little secret. I heard everything and saw him drop the money. If he had nothing to hide, he wouldn't have run away. A common thief is all he is and now he's going to pay the price for stealing. Now, I'll tell you one more time. Move out of the way or I will knock you out of the way".

Charlie's voice was so quiet and threatening that it took every ounce of her courage not to move. Abigail was terrified that if Charlie got hold of the boy, he would do him serious damage. She could still vividly remember the time her husband had punched her arm and if Charlie hit John as hard as she had been hit, the boy could end up with broken bones or even dead.

As Charlie grabbed his wife's arm with one hand, he slapped her face with the other and shoved her to one side. He kept hold of Abigail until he had gripped John by the neck of his shirt and began dragging the boy towards the stairs. Hannah was screaming and as Charlie passed her in the hallway slapped her face so hard with the back of his hand that she spun round and ended up in a heap on the carpet.

Abigail ran to her daughter and picked her up, wondering what Hannah was doing on the floor. "Mum, go and help John, he's going to kill him. Mum, you have to stop him. Dad's going to kill him!" Hannah pleaded.

When Abigail didn't move, Hannah shook herself free from her mother's arms and raced up the stairs. John had stopped screaming but Hannah could still hear the sound of leather slapping over and over again. As she jumped onto her father's back, Charlie turned around and Hannah fell to the floor. She pulled herself up and stared at this man who was meant to be her father, and Charlie dropped the belt he had used on his son and ran out of the bedroom.

****

The car pulled onto the drive and John got out of the passenger's side before Charlie had turned the engine off. The boy ignored his mother and went straight upstairs. When Charlie came through the back door into the kitchen, Abigail looked at her husband waiting for him to speak like she always did.

"John won't touch another thing that doesn't belong to him. He now knows what the inside of a cell looks like and he's had a right grilling from the sergeant. He won't be going back to St. Bede's and he's got the rest of the week off school so I expect that you stay in and look after him. He's not allowed out of this house until he starts at St Joseph's, just up the road. You can look for a job next week," Charlie said. "Oh, and he blamed me because of being a policeman would you believe? Some story of him being bullied at the school and forced to hand over money to two brothers or else he would be beaten. These two have also been dealt with and I wasn't a bit surprised to find out they came from a bad lot. I locked up their father the other week and the two lads said it was payback for that but John has to understand that my role in the community is to keep scum like them under control and he has not to sink to their level."

Abigail nodded at her husband and turned her attention to the chip pan, dropping the cut potato into the hot fat. "Tea will be twenty minutes," was all she said and Charlie walked into the parlour after hanging his police tunic up on a hook by the kitchen door.

Poor John being bullied, she thought as she looked for more painkillers. Her head was aching and had been since she got up this morning. It was strange thought Abigail; she knew there had been other things happening today. John going for a run early this morning was peculiar. Hannah off school with a strange mark on her face and saying she had a tummy ache, John going to work with Charlie and now Charlie saying stupid things about thieves. It made no sense to her at all and she just wished that her memory would stop playing tricks on her, making her forget what was happening. Well whatever happened today can't have been all that bad. As she swallowed the first tablet with a mouthful of water, throwing her head back to make sure the tiny white disc didn't stick in her throat, Abigail's vision went blurry and she clung to the sink until she could see just one of everything and not two.

Charlie couldn't stand being in the house. Tea had been eaten in silence and John had kept his head bent so that he didn't have to look at him as they ate. Abigail had chattered incessantly about their holiday in Scotland, unaware that no-one was answering her. Hannah, however, had looked him straight in the eye when he asked how her day had been at school. Her reply was measured and her voice steady as she told him that she hadn't been to school due to a red hand mark on her face.

The girl had stared at him with hatred blazing from her eyes and Charlie had stood up from the table and told Abigail he was going back to work. His daughter had infuriated him and Charlie knew better than to do what he wanted to do. He wanted to slap her face so hard that she wouldn't be able to speak for a week. How dare this child challenge him? Charlie would let it go this time as deep down he was relieved that with Hannah not going to school it meant no awkward questions had been asked by Hannah's teacher. It had been plain to see that the slap was no accident and Hannah was sometimes a bit too chatty. The last thing he needed was his daughter to talk about the carry on. In fact, .
no-one was going to mention it again.

"I expect that what happened today is never mentioned again and as from tomorrow, we carry on as though it never happened. If I find out anyone has spoken about a thief in this
house, or that the thief and those who protected him were hit as part of punishment that, by the way, any person who steals deserves, then those who talk will be in serious trouble. Do I make myself clear?" Charlie calmly asked before he walked out of the room and went back to work. He didn't need to hear the answer from his family as they knew what they were up against if they breathed a word about what happened in this house to the outside world, even to each other.

Abigail smiled at her children and said, "Take no notice of your Dad. There's no thief been in this house and as for hitting you two, well, I know he loves you too much and would never harm a hair on your heads. Now, if you have both finished your tea, you can go and do the washing up. John, you wash and Hannah, you wipe and put away. I have a headache and need to sit quiet for a bit."

Chapter 18.

Charlie had got a promotion. It was only a promotion of sorts as he was still classed as a constable within the police but it was definitely a step on another ladder, a new ladder to climb as he had been informed that he was to be the first ever police detective in the small town of Formby. Charlie was ecstatic.

It meant moving house again and for Charlie, it couldn't come quickly enough. Formby was an area that was known for people with status. Footballers who played for both the Liverpool and Everton teams lived in Formby as well as doctors, school teachers and many other middle-class professionals. Charlie felt as though he had just won the pools, so great was his joy.

There were more private houses than council houses and there was a golf club that was second only to Royal Birkdale golf club that was only a few miles away. Charlie had decided that when they moved, this would become his latest sporting activity as he would be mixing with the famous, the wealthy and best of all had the added bonus of being in a newly made position that reeked of importance. People would want to meet him and he would make sure
that he was meeting the right type of people, the people that he had aspired to be like for so many years.

A Detective was head and shoulders above an ordinary policeman where pounding the beat was as good as it got. Charlie grinned at his reflection in the mirror that was propped up on the kitchen windowsill and began his daily ritual that always started with a shave.

Detective Constable Charles Hennessey, as he would be known very soon cursed loudly as the razor jagged and his chin turned red from the sharp cut. As he rinsed his face and tore a piece of newspaper to stick on the still bleeding nicked skin, he decided to wait to tell Abigail about the move until he got home tonight. No need to have her upset too soon as it would be so difficult for her to leave this place behind. Abigail loved living in Thornton and deep down, Charlie was concerned that she would not be able to rise to the higher standards of life in Formby.

He would need to pick his moment to drop this bombshell carefully. Abigail knew that it was all part of being a policeman's wife, being transferred to a different area but she was so settled and happy, Charlie was concerned that it might throw her into another brain meltdown as he called it.

Abigail would have to cope with a new house, find another job, find people to pass the time of day with and most importantly not let him down when he brought his new, more respectable friends to his home for a few drinks after a round of golf. He smiled at his reflection as he gently peeled the stuck newspaper from his chin, wondering who would be his first important guest to his new, middle class home.

****

Abigail had no choice.
She had to move and that was that.

A better life her husband, who now demanded to be called Charles, said. More prospects for the children as living in a more affluent area opened up more possibilities. They would mix with the good and the great of the town and Charlie, as she still called him, was determined it would happen.
Trust him, he had said, it would be a wonderful place to live.

He had already enrolled Hannah into the local Girl Guide group that was attached to the school at which she would finish her junior education. Our Lady's, it was called. It had small classes so Hannah would get the best of attention and be even more intelligent than she already was. It was grammar school for her in a year, Charlie had said and then that girl will have the world at her feet. All down to him, he added.

John had been sorted out with a weekend job in the petrol station right across the road from their new house and would be serving petrol to the locals. He would be able to work with what he still loved since being a toddler, cars. In time, Charlie was sure that John would be a mechanic. Now that was a job for life and would bring him into contact with all the right people too. Charlie would make it happen, he said.

As Charlie enthusiastically talked of the future, Abigail wondered if his big plans for the children would become a reality or would the reality be that they would escape his clutches as soon as they were old enough and become a huge embarrassment and disappointment to him, just like she knew she was. After all, that's what he often told her and she had come to believe his words.

For now, Abigail knew that her best option was to agree with everything he was saying and to match his enthusiasm about being posher all because of a few big houses, the odd football player and his bloody sideways promotion to a Detective.

****

The house stood on Liverpool Road and was one of four semi-detached police houses. There was a long path that ran the length of the land, from the gate, past the back door and down to a separate garage that was allocated to this house. A beautiful climbing plant that had been left by the previous family was somehow anchored to the wall by the front door and the front garden was well-maintained - pretty flowers filled the borders that lined the immaculately mown lawn.

Abigail had to admit, it looked so nice from the outside and was quite looking forward to seeing what the inside had to offer. Inside of the house was wonderful, Abigail exclaimed. They had all gone into the house by the back door and the first thing they saw was a proper cloakroom. Pegs stood proudly above a built-in bench so that once you had hung up your coat, you could sit to take off your footwear and tidy them away underneath this seating. There was also a huge set of cupboards for storing things in and best of all, a downstairs toilet completed this space. What luxury, Abigail thought as she admired the cream floor tiles that were fitted perfectly. This beats an old out house any day.

As Charles opened a door, Abigail was looking at the biggest kitchen she had ever seen in any semi- detached house. This was bigger than the parlour and kitchen combined in the house in Thornton and Abigail was hooked. No more trailing plates from one room to another as this was big enough to put in the table and chairs that were shoved into the corner of parlour at Thornton. The set would fit easily in the middle of the floor and there would still be masses of space to move freely, she laughed happily.

"Oh Charlie, oops, Charles," Abigail corrected herself, "I love it already and yes, you were right. It's just perfect and so light and modern. Oh, that downstairs toilet is the height of luxury and look at all the room!".

As Abigail went around the rest of the house exclaiming loudly at this and that, Charles smiled. His wife was going to be fine in Formby and he would have no problems turning her
into a middle-class housewife who complemented the requirements for his way of living.

He might even get her a twin tub washing machine. Now that would show the neighbours that he was a good provider to his wife and children and after all, she would have much more to wash when he got the necessary clothes that a Detective needed. No more blue uniform for Charles Hennessey.

As he puffed out his chest with delight, he thought about the seamstress in the small shop who he had met in the quaint shopping area known as "The Village". He couldn't wait for her to measure him up for a couple of hand made suits and maybe she would be up for measuring his inside leg in private. Well, if she offered, who was he to refuse a lady?

Chapter 19.

Abigail was lonely since the move from Thornton to Formby. Her neighbours were nice people but kept themselves to themselves and Abigail felt as though they only tolerated her because it was a neighbourly thing to do.

She had made friends with a woman who worked in a greengrocer's shop on Redgate and on occasion Abigail invited her for a cuppa when she knew that Charles was not home for lunch as it was now called, as he was in court giving evidence against a wrongdoer.

Suzanne and Abigail had been getting quite friendly and eventually, Abigail had plucked up the courage to tell Charlie that she had made a friend. At first, he was annoyed but when he had done some digging and found out who this woman was, he agreed that Abigail could bring her to the house for a chat. After all, Suzanne's husband was the treasurer at Formby Golf Club so, because he was an honest man and one of standing, the friendship was allowed to continue. It became a weekly treat for Abigail and she looked forward to having a bit of adult company, well, women's company, as all she had the rest of the week was the children to talk to if they could be bothered to spend any time with her.

Abigail had noticed that both the children were growing distant with each year that passed and when their father was at home were desperate to be given permission to call on their own friends. If they were refused permission by Charles to leave the house, neither of them would speak unless it was absolutely necessary but made sure that they were very polite to him as he insisted that they all sat together to watch the television and have some family time.

Funny, thought Abigail, they both had a set of friends but John and Hannah never brought anyone home and they always called to their friends' houses. It was a rare event if a friend called for her children to go out somewhere since they had moved. After all, Charles was always wonderful with anyone of the children's mates who called when they lived in Thornton. He took great pains to get to know each one. It was always the same procedure asked in such a friendly way.

Name, age, address, father's occupation, mother's occupation, brothers and sisters.

Charles was always happy to get to know who his children were associated with and Abigail had no idea that he was vetting the whole family of each child who came calling, for any criminal activity. If anything turned up, then he made sure that the friendship his children had built was ended.

John and Hannah, on the other hand were well aware of what was happening and ran the gauntlet of being left out of street games that were played endlessly on the estate up the road by gangs of happy, friendly children.

When they had moved to Formby, they had both decided never to bring anyone round if their father was home and became very selective who could meet their mother too. If she was having a bad time with remembering, it got so awkward when she constantly asked, "Have I met you before?" John and Hannah were terrified to explain what was happening in their home to anyone in case it got back to their father and he hit them again.

Suzanne had told Abigail about a job that was available in a pet shop on the outskirts of Formby. It was a full-time job that included Saturdays but, like all shops, was closed for half a day on Thursdays. It was a friend of Suzanne's who owned it, well her friend's husband, and she had asked her to look out for someone to replace the man who was retiring.

"Heavy lifting, sacks of animal feed to hump from the storeroom to the shop and you have to lock the shop up if you want to go to the toilet. It's an old outside lavvy at the end of the yard and you have to clean it once a week. You'll be on your own and basically run the place. The only time you see anyone is when they come to open up in a morning and let you away at night. What do you think Abigail?" Suzanne asked her friend.

Abigail wasn't sure how Charlie would react to her working full time but the money would be good and Hannah was old enough to come in from school and start preparing tea. She was thirteen now and more than capable of being left on her own until she got home.

Anyway, Charlie had been on her case about a job again and this would hopefully please him. Part-time work for a lady from a middle-class area was what he had insisted she found. No cleaning and no bar work even though these jobs were plentiful. A shop job was what she had to focus on getting.

"Yes, I'll have it, if they want me," Abigail smiled. "Can you let me know when they will want to see me about it? I can't go tomorrow, it's wash day".

Suzanne grinned at her friend. Abigail was a lovely person and it would do her good to have a bit of independence. Although Abigail never said one wrong word about her husband, Suzanne guessed that she had a hard time and he was the cause of it.

"Pop into the grocer's tomorrow morning, first thing before we get busy and I'll tell you then. It'll give you time to do your washing without interruption when you get back. Oh, a word of warning, my friend is lovely but her husband, Mr Billington is a bit funny. Just don't go in the store room with him or if you have to, keep the door open. He's rumoured to have roaming eyes and wandering hands so just watch yourself. See you tomorrow Abigail. Thanks for the cuppa, love, but I'll have to go now. I'll be late back otherwise".

The two women laughed as Abigail retorted if Mr Billington as much as breathed on her, she'd throw the nearest sack at him and hit him on the head with the weighing scale pan.

Abigail saw her friend out of the house and hugged herself. "Sod Charles," she said. "I'm taking this job if they offer it to me and for once, I will do what I want, not what he says."

Chapter 20.

Abigail was weighing out the dog biscuits and packing them into brown bags. She had to stick down the top of the bag with sticky tape and then write on the front of the bag the name of the biscuits and the price with a black marker pen. Then they went onto a shelf in exactly the right place. These bags had to weigh a pound and eight ounces and as she looked for the weights she needed to put on the scales, the shop door opened. The bell tinkled and the pet parrot that sat in his huge cage that was suspended from the ceiling shouted, "All right mate!" in a broad Liverpudlian accent.

It was a young boy who had come into the shop. He was wearing a beautiful green blazer that covered the whitest shirt Abigail had ever seen and a school tie that she didn't recognise as belonging to any school locally. He had long grey trousers on with a perfectly ironed crease that would slice your finger open if you ran your finger down it.

"Do you buy pets?" he asked Abigail and his eyes suddenly filled with tears that he hurriedly brushed away on the sleeve of his blazer.

"No love, we don't. Well, we do, but only from a supplier not from ordinary people and we only sell rabbits and hamsters. What do you want to sell? Is it a load of white mice that have suddenly multiplied?" Abigail asked as she caught sight of a small cage that the boy was carrying.

The boy shook his head. "It's my hamster. I have to find her a new home. I'm going to boarding school and I can't take her. My parents have refused to look after her so I need to find her a new home today."

As the tears began to trickle down his face, Abigail came from behind the counter and asked to see the pet. She lifted the cage onto the counter and asked if the hamster was tame. The boy nodded and Abigail encouraged him to get the creature out of its cage.

The hamster sat quietly in the boy's hand and when Abigail asked if she could hold Queenie, the name the boy had given this animal, the boy handed his beloved pet to her. Abigail was amazed at how warm and soft this little hamster was and told the boy that she would take Queenie. The hamster could be a pet for Hannah and Abigail promised to look after her properly until her daughter learned what to do with a hamster.

"Would a pound be enough to buy her?" Abigail asked the boy. "I can't spare any more than that.".

He nodded and took Queenie and returned her to the cage. He was still upset but looked relieved that his pet was safe. Abigail gave him a pound note from her purse and told the boy to stay as long as he wanted to say goodbye.

A car horn sounded and the boy in the beautiful uniform turned and ran out of the shop.

Another mouth to feed, Abigail sighed as she took a packet of hamster food from the shelf and dropped twenty pence into the till. Now how on earth was she going to pay the catalogue bill this month? And the Provi loan woman was due tomorrow. She reached into the cage and lifted out the tame, furry creature. "It doesn't matter," she murmured. "I'll go into town on half day closing and pay the outstanding amount on the coupons at their office." Then, returning the new pet to its cage, began to weigh out the dog biscuits.

****

It was pay day. It was always on half day closing and Abigail had never been as glad to see a pay packet in her life. She had managed to keep her debtors at bay but knew that if she missed getting into town and to the head office of the loan company, there would be no more leeway with missed payments and she would have to tell Charles and face his wrath once again. Abigail had agreed to clear the arrears today and it would leave a huge hole in this month's housekeeping but she had no choice if she was to stop her husband finding out.

Abigail's wage packet was on the counter when she got into the pet shop but she left it where it was. It was a ritual that had to be followed whereby Mr Billington firstly checked the stock, made a note of what needed ordering from the wholesalers and cleaned out the parrot cage. Abigail always felt uncomfortable as his small dark eyes seemed to be looking at her chest when he spoke to her. Parrot Eyes Billington, Abigail had laughed with Suzanne, when her friend had asked how the job was going and if His Nibs was behaving.

The bird was allowed to fly around the shop today and Abigail loved to see its colourful plumage close up as it waddled across the counter towards her. Abigail had only tried to stroke the bird once and had ended up with a nasty cut as the bird pecked her viciously and took a chunk out of her finger. As the parrot looked at her with a beady eye, head on one side, she took a step back.

"Oh, nice bum, Mrs Hennessey," her boss said. As she had stepped back, Abigail hadn't realised Mr Billington had been behind her and she had bumped into him. Horrified, Abigail went to get away but he grabbed her and squeezed her hard on her bottom. Abigail spun round and slapped him soundly on his face.

"Don't you dare touch me again or I'll tell my husband. Then you'll know what a squeeze is," she hissed at this man whose eyes were as beady as the parrot's. "I was warned about you and now I'm warning you, keep your hands to yourself if you know what's good for you. You won't be able to squeeze a wet sponge out if Charles gets hold of you".

Mr Billington glared angrily at Abigail. "It was only a bit of fun and let's face it, your husband is always up for a bit of fun. In fact, he seems to be having quite a bit of fun lately." His beady eyes shone brightly as Abigail stared in disbelief at the shop owner. "So, I just thought you might be feeling a bit neglected, like, that you brushed up against me on purpose, you know, to feel wanted. And as the good employer I am, I have to look after my staff. Now, Abigail, let's forget about this. After all, no harm done eh? Oh, and you can take your pay packet now. Everything has tallied so there won't be any deductions," he said nervously.

He patted his shoulder, and the parrot flew round the shop and landed with ease where Mr Billington had indicated. He held out his hand and the bird made its way down his arm to get the treat that was waiting and whilst the parrot ate, the shop owner put the parrot into its home. Once the bird was safely in the clean cage, he walked out of the shop, smiling to himself.

Time for a new shop assistant or better still his bloody wife could get in here and run the damned place. Now how could he get rid of this woman, and quickly? In fact, today would be perfect. Nobody threatened him with the law and the last thing he wanted was for people to stop coming to the shop. Things were tight enough as it was, financially. He was being undercut on so many products as the supermarkets that were springing up could sell much cheaper than him. Abigail Hennessey would have to go. He would save a wage and get rid of any trouble that might head his way if his wife was in here. As his conscience pricked him over letting her believe her husband was being unfaithful as a way of saving himself, he vowed never to employ a woman again. Too much trouble by half and his own wife gave him plenty of that now that the takings were down. There was more to come once he told her she had to earn a living instead of freeloading off him.

****

Charles Hennessey asked her again. "Where did you leave your pay packet? Are you sure it was in your shopping bag? Who else has been in the storeroom Abigail? It can't just vanish you know." He looked so professional in his office in the police station and Abigail felt so small and intimidated as her husband grilled her for answers.

She felt as though she was going to vomit. Her money had gone. The whole lot. She usually put her earnings into her purse but with all the commotion first thing, Abigail hadn't been thinking clearly. She was just so relieved that there had been no deductions this week as the till had been right. Not one penny short. Not one penny over. As she realised what she had said, Abigail watched her husband's face drain of colour.

It was funny how the till was always wrong when that boy of the Billington's was around and he hadn't been in all this week. Abigail had had her suspicions but couldn't prove anything as Mr Billington allowed his son to take ten pence every day for sweets from the till after school and she was sure he was taking a bit more some days. Usually the only day the boy wasn't in was Thursday but this week the boy had been ill with something or other and hadn't been to school and the till was right. It made no odds though, even if she said anything, Mr Billington's boy would not be asked if it was him as he was spoiled rotten and could do no wrong.

Strange how they hadn't accused her of pilfering, Abigail had often thought but she had agreed that any shortfall in the takings was her responsibility and would be deducted from her pay when she took the job. It wasn't huge amounts that she lost but any loss was never good and fifty pence down every week added up to a lot of money in a month. It was the price of her loan and in effect, she was paying it twice.

"The only person who has been in is Mr Billington. First thing as normal and then to use the toilet at the end of the yard around eleven o'clock. Said he got caught short as he'd had one cuppa too many with the wholesaler. He came back to lock up at lunch time and all he did was go behind the counter and told me to go. I wouldn't have noticed it gone but when I went to get bus fare out of my purse, I realised I'd left the packet in my bag. When I couldn't find it, I came straight in here to you."

Charlie looked through the Yellow Pages for the telephone number of the pet shop and dialled the number. It was answered almost immediately.

"D.C. Charles Hennessey here from Formby police, is that Mr Billington? Ah Mr Billington, it seems as though you have had a sneak thief in your shop today and I am coming to talk to you now. No, Mr Billington, you will wait. I will be five minutes."

As Charles told Abigail to go to the car, he patted her arm. "He will give you every penny he owes you including the deductions he thinks he can make for his till being short before we leave. He can claim on his insurance for the theft unless, of course, it's something to do with Mr Big Boy Billington and then he will be getting his collar felt. Now, don't you worry, I'll soon have this sorted out."

As she sat in the car, Charles suddenly asked Abigail, "Has he ever tried anything on with you Abigail, you know, flirting or that? He's not well liked at the golf club as he's always coming on strong with the women and he's been warned by the committee to stop or leave. One of the uniforms had to go and have a word yesterday at his house and I was going to talk to you about it at home later on. No wife of mine is working for such a sleaze as him, so when we have your money, just understand that you won't be going back to work for him again and not just because of the wages."

Abigail's face crumpled and she managed to whisper, "No Charles, he hasn't but please let me carry on working until I get another job. I have got used to the money and you know how much easier it is with both of us working. I'll look for something else but please, let me stay."

There was going to be enough trouble and Abigail was terrified of what her boss would say about Charles being unfaithful to his face if she said yes about this morning's carry on. Abigail couldn't bear another affair to be uncovered. Her life was so stable at the moment, apart from a bit of debt and she was managing to keep it from Charles and that was enough for her to worry about. She had a feeling that if he did meet someone else, he would leave her.

After all, Hannah was nearly fourteen and was leaving school soon. Charles was insisting Hannah got a Saturday job and contributed to the house just like John was. If Hannah wanted to go to college, then the girl had to fund it herself.

His parenting days were nearly done and Charles had commented it was nearly time for him to live his life without supporting them, the children, for much longer. It had hurt Abigail that her husband only said him and not both of them and this had set her mind racing despite not having any proof he was going to leave her.

****

Chapter 21.

"Seven mornings a week. Half nine to eleven o'clock. Start tomorrow at nine and my wife will show you the ropes. It'll only take a few days for you to get into the routine and the other girl who cleans will keep you right too. You both have your own set jobs and she brings her kid along but he's no trouble. Lovely little lad who just sits in his pushchair. Now, I've got to go, the dray men are here with my delivery. See you in the morning Abigail."

The job Abigail got was in the The Royal Hotel over the road from her house. Charles had agreed to it as the landlord had approached him in person when he had called in on police business. Charles wasn't too pleased to have been approached but felt he had no choice but to say yes.

His wife was bleeding him dry since he had made her give up her job in the pet shop and as it was his doing, he had no choice but to give her extra money. He had even bitten his tongue when she said about the bloody coupons that she was paying back at an extortionate rate of interest every week. A necessity, she had said, as spreading the cost was easier than saving up for something and she used most of it for Christmas as he refused to help her out.
His wife had got far too confident for her own good since she had had a taste of freedom and he hated the fact.

The Royal, as it was known, was a favourite of the locals and had a bar area with a linoleum covered floor, rough wooden tables and stools and a long settee that ran the length of one wall. Nothing fancy but when you considered it was used by the men who came straight from work and were often dirty from their manual jobs, fancy was not needed. Just somewhere to sit, a dart board and a smiling face behind the bar to take away the stress of the day's work.

The second room was known as the Blue Room and as its name suggested was decorated in a deep luxurious blue. Carpeted and warm, this was a great place for the younger generation to meet as there was a juke box that was updated regularly with the chart-topping songs and they could enjoy themselves and meet friends, maybe get a date with someone and relax with people of their own age. There were groups of young ladies and young men who would enjoy a few drinks on a Friday and Saturday night before heading off to one of the nightclubs either in the town itself or to Tiffany's in Ainsdale that was a short bus ride away.

The lounge bar was designed in red and gold to reflect the brewery colours. All Bass Charrington houses kept to the same format and this space was used more by couples and groups and more mature men and when there was a family get together, there was space and luxury to help the customers enjoy their celebrations.

There was a beer garden that had been turned into a mini putting green as the Landlord was an avid golfer and all his golfing associates came to drink and practice their skills. To top it all off, there was an off licence that sold beer, wines and spirits to take away as well as a selection of cigarettes, crisps and sweets, a little shop that was separate from the pub where the teenagers pushed their luck trying to buy cider to drink at the park.

Eric ran a good house and his quick sense of humour and easy way made him a popular figure in Formby. He called everybody 'Dad', but no-one knew why. People just accepted his strange greeting and never took any offence, even if you were a woman. Winnie, his wife, was a quiet woman who no-one would mess with. She had a tongue so sharp that if you upset her or behaved badly in her husband's pub, it wasn't too long before you made your excuses and left. Her straight talking had everyone showing her the utmost respect even though usually she was quiet and liked to be in the background.

They complemented each other despite being so different and even though they were a married couple, were not often seen as a partnership where the running of the pub was concerned. Eric was the perfect host and Winnie only showed her face in the bars when it was absolutely necessary. Usually it was when they were short staffed or if there was any trouble, which on both counts, was not often.

****

Abigail loved her job. She had made friends with Eileen who worked with her and adored Eileen's son. They had taken to visiting each other's houses for a natter and for some reason, Charles had not interfered.

In fact, he had been more than happy to have Eileen at his home. At least if his wife had company, she didn't bother him too much. It was taking Charles all his time to be in the same room as Abigail and to keep a civil tongue but he was always pleasant and friendly when Eileen was around. She would need a friend once he had gone. Fifteen years was up in eighteen months and like he had vowed, all those years ago, he was waiting to get his life back and do his own thing. Not much longer now. All he had to do was find someone to share
his bed occasionally, someone who was not demanding and liked to have a good time. Someone normal.

****

Abigail was oblivious to her husband's plan and as far as she was concerned her marriage had survived. Now that John had left home and Hannah was nearly ready to leave school, she was looking forward to building a new future with more time spent with Charles. He would be less stressed as they could do things together now that Hannah could be left on her own and was more than competent to fend for herself.

Abigail wasn't lonely any more since she had become friends with Eileen Geoffrey who was down to earth and ordinary. She was just like the people of Thornton who Abigail got on so well with and Eileen, despite being ten years her junior was so easy to be with. Eileen was a good friend and Abigail knew it was a friendship that would last forever. Eileen didn't mind if Abigail's house was messy or if Hannah sat and talked with them when her daughter was on school holidays. Eileen took everyone just as they were and was always funny, kind and caring.

When Eileen said she was leaving The Royal to have another baby, Abigail was distraught. The two of them worked so well together and it wouldn't be the same not having anyone to laugh with and if Eric didn't get anyone else to replace her dear friend, it would be double the work. Maybe she would get more money if she did more work. Every cloud, thought Abigail sadly but at least Eileen wasn't moving away so they would still be friends and help each other out whenever possible and she was looking forward to the arrival of the new baby so much.

Eileen's little boy called her Auntie Ab and no doubt this little baby would do the same in time. Eileen was more like family than Abigail's real family were and she loved her status as surrogate auntie. In fact, she didn't feel like a surrogate auntie as Eileen included Abigail in so many areas of her family life. Bonfire parties with her brothers and their families, Christmas parties where Hannah was always welcomed too and those long hot summer afternoons, sitting in the garden watching the boy play happily whilst they drank endless cups of tea and put the world to rights. Abigail felt as though she fitted somewhere at long last and Eileen's husband was one of the nicest men she had ever met. If only her husband was like him, life would be a breeze, she thought.

****

It was nearly Christmas and Abigail and her daughter were looking through the catalogue for clothes for Hannah. Hannah wanted all the latest fashionable clothes and Abigail was trying to persuade her to look at items that were not too over the top. Charles would go mad with her if Hannah was overly fashionable and thankfully, Hannah had eventually decided on a pair of high waisted trousers with a large elasticated clasp belt and a polo neck jumper.

John was to have a pair of denim flares and a jumper with some sort of picture knitted in the front and Abigail had found a brown checked dress with three quarter sleeves and a cream cardigan that would do for Christmas day and then be used for best. Nothing too outrageous but still smart and serviceable for all of them.

Abigail had got Charles a machine that, if you got the golf ball into the right place, the machine fired the ball back to you. It was to help with putting on a golf course, so the advert on the television said. Abigail had been saving Green Shield stamps and had enough to claim this present that she hoped he would like. Anyway, if he liked the present or not it was a relief that Abigail had not had to spend one penny on her husband. The children could have a bit more this year.

Charles had a new set of friends and Abigail was sick of him being at the golf club. He was never away from that blasted place and even on his days off, was out early in the morning and came rolling home stinking of drink late at night. When Abigail asked to be introduced to them, Charles had told her no.

When Abigail insisted on meeting his new friends, Charles suddenly got very angry. He said that she would not fit in with them and he was ashamed to be seen with her. He had berated her and called her a fat, useless woman who was a failure as a wife and then stormed out of the house before she had a chance to say anything.

Abigail sat wearily on the settee and wondered which one of the friends was Charles's bit on the side. She knew the signs, after all, she was a professional in the ways of Charles Hennessey and his dalliances. Abigail would no doubt find out who his latest conquest was soon enough.

"Ah, well," she muttered as she hauled herself up and went to find the two packets of crisps and bottle of coke she had taken from the pub and would pay for on pay day. She owed a fortune as this little treat had become a daily habit. Eating those lovely crisps and washing them down with a fizzy drink made Abigail feel comforted and she needed so much comfort from somewhere right now. She would start a diet tomorrow.

Chapter 22.

Christmas Day 1974 was just like any other day in the Hennessey household in as much as it had to be geared around what Charles insisted on.

Abigail was listening to Christmas carols on the radiogram that Charles had bought, the latest must have accessory to the house. It was the best thing, he said, to play records on as it had stereo sound and made the music much better to listen to. She was polishing the furniture in the lounge until it gleamed and hoped that Charles came straight home and didn't pop into the Bay Horse pub that was near the police station for a quick drink. It would no doubt lead to a stay behind for the landlord's friends to enjoy his hospitality after closing time.

Last year, it was nearly tea time before they ate and Charles complained bitterly that the food was disgusting as it had been kept warm for so long. Needless to say, the day was a disaster and the meal was eaten in complete silence and the presents left unopened. Charles had fallen asleep in the lounge as soon as he had sat in front of the roaring coal fire, his glass of beer dropping onto the carpet as his drink fuelled sleep relaxed his grip. He had to finish the drink before they got their treats as was the norm and now, the head of the house was asleep, everyone knew better than to disturb him.

Abigail and the children had sat well into the evening before he woke and when they eventually got their gifts, Charles had yelled at them for being ungrateful as they didn't thank him properly then promptly picked himself up and went back to the pub and the party that he had been loathe to leave. It would be in full swing now and he was looking forward to a bit of merrymaking. Even better as it was free drink as the pubs were not licensed to sell on Christmas night.

Anything was better than being in this house he had told them. Miserable, ungrateful family was what he had spat out, and said that they should be thankful for what he provided. When the back door slammed shut, Abigail looked forlornly at her children as they both said they were going to bed. Once they had left the room, she allowed the tears to fall silently. The twinkling fairy lights on the tree blurred into a myriad of colours as she stared at them. Like a rainbow, Abigail thought, but with no lucky pot of gold at the end of it, well not for her.

****

Hannah was peeling potatoes and grumbling that she didn't want to go to church and if her mother wasn't going then neither would she. John was still in bed and refusing to get up, claiming he would come down soon, once his headache had gone from his one too many
pints of mixed mild ale and bitter beer. John had come back to live with them when his flatmate had moved and he couldn't afford the rent, much to Charles's disgust.

As the LP stopped, Abigail went to turn the disc over and smiled happily as she lifted the lid on the radiogram. This side had her favourites on it and as the sound of "Silent Night" began, Abigail sang at the top of her voice and felt, like the words she sung, calm and bright and almost happy.

Once the hymn had finished and a new tune began, Abigail went to check the turkey. One more basting and it would be ready she decided. Her mouth watered as she anticipated her
plate piled high with all the delights that came with a Christmas feast, especially the Christmas pudding that she managed to cram in no matter how full she was from the main meal.

A knock on the front door broke into her thoughts and she instructed Hannah to go and see who was calling, today of all days.

"Tell them your Dad is at work and will be back in an hour or so, Hannah. If they need to speak with him, he's at the station," she told her daughter as she returned the turkey to the oven.

"It's Dad," Hannah told to her mother. "He's looking drunk and there's some other people with him who are just as bad. I'm stopping in here until they've gone." She sat down at the table that was littered with potato peelings, a sulky expression on her face.

Abigail sighed. She was not ready for visitors as she was still wearing her ordinary clothes and had done nothing with her hair. She quickly shut the kitchen door and waited until she heard Charles usher his guests into the lounge. Then she bolted upstairs to get changed and make herself presentable so that Charles would not be embarrassed. He was home an hour early and Abigail was not pleased. Her routine had been broken and she was unsure how to fit in everything else she had to do now that she had to entertain these people. Guests or not, Charles would expect his meal immediately when they went.

When she came downstairs, there was laughter coming from the lounge and Abigail steeled herself before she went in. Who were these people and why had Charles not introduced her as soon as they came in? He usually did, even though he knew she would not be dressed to his standards when he sometimes brought home unexpected visitors.

As she opened the door, the laughter stopped abruptly and Charles told her to go and turn off the dinner. "We will eat when my friends have gone, once we have had a few whiskies and their lift arrives to take them home. A couple of hours Abigail, that's all. Oh, and seeing though you don't drink whiskey, you'd better get yourself a lemonade if you want to join us. Can't be in here without a glass in your hand." He grinned at these people and they all laughed heartily as she turned to go back into the kitchen and he picked up the bottle to refill his glass.

Abigail eventually went back to where this impromptu party was now in full swing. Charles was squashed in between two women on the settee and she saw her husband quickly remove his hand from the knee of one of them. He stared at his wife defiantly and then introduced Abigail.

"Everyone, this is the woman who cooks and keeps house for me, I suppose I should say, my wife."

As Charles continued to stare at her, one of the men sniggered and drunkenly muttered, "Hmm, for now," and a deathly silence suddenly filled the room.

****

The rest of the day was a disaster. Abigail had forgotten to turn the oven off and the turkey was overcooked and dry. Charles complained that she was totally useless. Hannah refused to eat anything and sat sullenly until she jumped up and announced she was going to her room. John had eaten his meal in silence and then left the table to go back to bed. Abigail had tried to keep the conversation going but eventually, she gave up and pushed her food around the plate, waiting for Charles to leave her on her own.

When he stood to leave the table he grumbled, "Ungrateful little bastards. That's the last Christmas I spend here if that's their attitude." Then he stumbled out of the kitchen. "I'm going for a kip on the settee, so keep the noise down on that telly if you know what's good for you."

As she cleared the table and filled the sink with water, her tears dropped steadily onto the bubbles that were forming and Abigail wondered if she would ever feel happiness again at this special time of year and if Charles meant what he had said.

Chapter 23.

It was a month before Hannah's fifteenth birthday and Charles Hennessey had something to tell them. Well, his version at least.

"I'm moving out at the end of the week and I won't be coming back. We have decided to get a divorce, me and your mum, but I'll still get to see you both. I want you to come to my new flat in Southport once I have got settled. Now don't get upset, it's for the best."

His voice trailed off as he looked at the faces of his children who sat stony-faced and totally uninterested in what he had told them.

Abigail sat with her head bent, unable to look at either child as she knew that she would break down completely and that they might see the swelling on her cheek. She had hidden so much from them, these two youngsters, as she still thought of them and needed to hide this mark that proved without doubt what a horrible man Charles really was.

John was a man himself now, granted, still a young man but he had lost that look and mis-shape of a youth still growing. He had filled out to be strong and muscled and the last time Charles had tried to discipline him and threatened another beating, her son had stood his ground and retaliated with such speed, force and venom behind the one punch he threw that it left Charles reeling.

Abigail had been secretly pleased that Charles had had a taste of his own medicine but felt so sad that it had come to this for her son and his father. John was still not the most talkative of people but his words chilled her to the bone when John calmly told Charles that he no longer had a father and that if he ever raised his hand to anyone in the house again, he would beat him to a pulp and gladly sit in a cell for as long as necessary. If her son saw the mark, she was terrified he would see his words through. After all, now Charles was going Abigail needed her son to help with the running of the house and to tell her what to do.

They may have to turn to him, one day, and although deep down Abigail knew that John and Hannah despised him, Charles was legally their father and he deserved to leave with a modicum of respect and she would not add to their feelings or thoughts. After all, the divorce was about man and wife, not the children.

"I'll be off to work then. See you tomorrow and if you want to talk about, well, if you want to, I'm here to listen," Charles Hennessey said lamely.

He quickly left the room when the silence became unbearable and despite his temper rising, he walked out with his head held high and his face straight so that he did not show any emotion whatsoever.

As he left the house, he breathed a sigh of relief. He had expected Hannah to cry and for John to storm out of the room. This silence had put him on the back foot and he wondered what the outcome would be for him from the two cuckoos he had brought to his nest and raised and when it would come. Everyone was changing and he had no idea when it had started and even less idea on how to stop it. He would think about that later. They would need him one day, those two supposed children of his but he would show them who was the boss when they came for help, especially John for whom he had a grudging respect, that was mixed with a touch of fear now that the lad had stood up to him. Best to leave John be and see what happened once things had settled down a bit. Charles was sure that if he threw enough money at the boy, it would make everything all right between them and Charles would then have a different hold on his bloody son and something else to throw at that woman he had as a wife for now, at least.

Let's see if they are prepared to support that mother of theirs, now he was going. They would soon need him when the money ran out and they didn't have two brass farthings to rub
together. At least they all knew better than to take this little matter outside of the four walls that was his home for only a few more days. He would get everything in order by the weekend and then he was off.

Once in the car, Charles smiled to himself and his thoughts quickly tumbled from family to lover. As he drove towards Southport, his mood lifted as he imagined the smile on his new love's face and the warm cuddle he would soon be sharing when she heard the good news that they were to be a proper couple. He stopped at the off licence for a bottle of whiskey, the same one that she had been drinking in his house on Christmas morning. It was a night to celebrate in style and like it or not, she was going to be exactly what he wanted her to be. After all, it was his lover's fault that he had to get divorced.

She wanted the trial run of three months as much as he did before they committed to a longer relationship and she would have to pay the price, one way or another now. It was as much her fault, in fact more, as she had moved herself into his new flat lock, stock and barrel and he had no way to get rid of her without throwing her onto the street, well for now. Anyway, sex was the best he had ever had so at least that was a bonus and Abigail, his stupid wife, would agree to anything. She always came around to his way of thinking.

Abigail wanted the divorce to be dealt with quickly. If truth be known, she didn't want a divorce at all but living like this was no longer an option either. Charles had told her he was going to live with this woman and Abigail had no way to stop him. Abigail had told him to divorce her and he had refused. Charles had said that if it didn't work out with his latest woman, then he would be back. Give him three months he had said and then he would be sure. He would pay the bills but not give her any housekeeping money until he decided. Charles was being reasonable and he insisted that Abigail had to be too. She had to do what he said.

Abigail refused.

Charles sensed that his hold over his wife was breaking but would not leave the matter alone. He had asked her civilly and when Abigail continued to refuse to agree, he had hit her across the face with the back of his hand.

Abigail left the house. She was closing the gate and heading up the road by the time Charles had realised she had had the audacity to walk out on him but he was not going to show himself up in public and bring her back. He wasn't sure if she would cause a scene. Abigail had changed and Charles felt as though he was on rocky ground. He would wait for her to come home and demand that she followed his orders and if it needed another slap to get her to agree, then so be it.

When she returned home, Charles was sat watching television and Abigail calmly dropped a piece of paper onto his lap.

"That's my solicitor's address and phone number. I have filed for divorce on the grounds of adultery and have named your fancy bit. I am more than happy to tell my solicitor more but that is now up to you. If you as much as blow breath on me the wrong way from this moment on, I will have you arrested and add it to my reasons for divorcing you. I want you out by the end of the week and you can tell the children tonight."

Then she turned and went into the kitchen to make tea. Hannah was due in from school soon and John would be home from work in an hour. "Funny," she said to herself, "I thought I would have had a headache by now," and she went to the fridge to get the minced beef.

Charles Hennessey stared at the piece of paper. He had been well and truly put in his place by Abigail and he knew he had no choice but to divorce her. He would have enough to deal with telling his superiors that his living arrangements were changing and if that stupid wife of his mentioned that he hit her, well, who knew where he would end up. He had blotted his copy book once too often and he might not be able to get away with this assault, especially as it could be seen by all and sundry.

It would cost a fortune, this divorce and as he folded the paper and pushed it into his pocket, he thought that maybe he should not have been too hasty with his demands of an open relationship. He had made his dream come true from all those years ago but not exactly as he had planned. Where would it leave him if this went horribly wrong? He couldn't control the woman who said she loved him but somehow seemed to love the whiskey bottle more.

****

The house was empty when he got up for the last time. Charles had been taking things to his new flat in Southport all week and had another two weeks to get everything he wanted out even though it was his last day under this roof. He was to give up his tenancy on the police house at the end of the month so could still walk in and out as he pleased and it was agreed that Abigail could continue to live there as long as she paid rent when he was no longer tied to the property.

Charles couldn't wait to get away and stay away. Two weeks would soon go by and as he was leaving Formby today, he was more than happy to tie up the loose ends from his new home in Southport. He had to pay off the outstanding utility bills to give Abigail a fresh start as he was still on the rent book, so to speak and it had made him mad to think that more money had to go and he had nothing to show for it. Despite the financial side niggling at him, somehow, he felt much more relaxed this morning and Charles Hennessey had a good feeling about the future.

He had been transferred to Southport police station and he had to go today to meet his new colleagues but was not worried by this. After all, he knew most of them already so it was just a formality and a new desk to him. The best thing was the opportunity to be involved with a higher class of sporting venue.

Royal Birkdale golf course was close by and he was very impressed with the people who frequented this place. It was one of the courses used for "The Open" golf tournament and it attracted so many rich, famous and talented golfers. Charles was looking forward to being
involved as he was sure he would be on duty at some point. He would find a way to wangle a round of golf there one day too. Much better than those people in Formby Golf Club, he thought as he heaved himself out of one of the twin beds that graced his marital bedroom. A cut above was that golf course.

At least he felt more like a proper man now he was having regular sex with his new partner and she was always willing after she had had a few drinks to relax her tired legs from standing in a shop all day. He had a spring in his step and was glad to have this house and time to himself for the last time ever to say goodbye and good riddance.

As his thoughts turned again to his new partner, he leered at himself as he caught his reflection in the mirror on the bathroom wall. No fear of any pregnancies too with this one as she had had a hysterectomy a few years ago when something went wrong in that department but at least she had had children so was a real woman. So, what if she had abandoned them to live with their grandparents when her marriage broke down and she had to get divorced? Nothing to do with Charlie boy, he smiled to himself as he realised, he had used her pet name for him and it felt good. As long as her brats didn't come to stop too often then that was good too. He'd done his bit where children were concerned. Life was good, mused Charles as he went to the sink to begin his morning routine

Chapter 24.

The divorce was done. Charles had not contested anything. Abigail had received her Decree Absolute and then those marriage vows that she had fought so hard to keep stood for nothing.

That was three years ago.

How sad it was that her life had come to this and despite being free from Charles and his controlling ways, Abigail was struggling to get through each day and it was getting steadily worse. It had been a struggle from the day he had left her for good.

He had been so happy to go and had not given her a second thought as he forged ahead with making a life with his new partner. Holidays, meals out in posh restaurants, new, fashionable clothes and Abigail was hurting to think that if he had been even a tiny bit kinder to her and the children, their lives would have been so much nicer. Charlie had everything and she had nothing.

She longed for the day he brought her maintenance money so that she could have a quick chat and look at the man she still loved despite his cruelty. It was always cash as she didn't have a bank account and when he left, Abigail hated herself for feeling the way she did. This was when she cried copious tears and ate whatever she bought from the shop on the corner for the rest of the day now she had some money.

Abigail was not too sure on how to run the house properly now that she was responsible for everything and when the quarterly bills began to arrive, there was never enough money to pay them. Abigail had let the housework slide and everywhere looked grubby and uncared for but no matter how hard she tried, she had no inclination to do anything unless it was watching the television or visiting Eileen. Even her cleaning job in The Royal was becoming hard work and she had been told off by Winnie for not doing her job to a good standard.

The bills were piling up. Red letters plopped onto the carpet almost every week and Abigail picked them up and stuffed them into a drawer in the sideboard. She didn't even bother to open them any more unless it was the electricity bill or the television licence. They had to be paid or how else would she be able to heat the lounge with the two-bar electric fire and what would she do if there was no television to watch? There was no gas supply to the house and she had to cook with electricity so this bill was a priority as was the television licence and the money to Radio Rentals each month at the showroom. If she didn't pay the rental on the telly, it would be repossessed and then she would have nothing nice in her life at all.

The coal house was empty apart from the dust and the merchant had refused her any more deliveries until she settled the last three months' payments. The telephone had been disconnected too and Abigail was so far behind with the rent that someone from the police had been to see her to set up a payment plan to pay on time and bring the arrears down. They had said if she missed another month, then they would take steps to get her evicted.

As she turned on the television and reached for a packet of crisps, Abigail wondered how long she had left living in this house. She sighed as she dragged the chair closer to the one bar that was glowing red and throwing the tiniest bit of heat out and it barely warmed her legs that were clad in laddered, nylon tights.

Charles had to pay maintenance for both her and Hannah and she had more money than she knew what to do with. He had to pay a fortune each month and as long as Hannah was in full time education, he was not able to reduce the payments. Abigail also got a little bit of state benefit and help with the rent too but somehow the money seemed to just vanish and she was unable to figure out how to make it stop. She was able to buy so many things that had only been a pipedream when she was married and it felt good to be able to treat herself to sweets each evening and huge bottles of fizzy drinks but her favourite was fish and chips or a huge Chinese meal on a Saturday night from the chippy near the village but for some reason, food and sweets were not making her happy any more and she was eating more and more to get that happy feeling but never quite managing to make it happen.

****

Hannah was at Southport Technical College. It was her second year and a new course.

She had wanted to be a secretary but had changed her mind when she couldn't buy the notepads, pencils and other equipment that was needed. She couldn't ask her Mum to help her as Abigail was always broke. Hannah wanted to leave to work full time in the Boulevard Restaurant on Lord Street where she did weekends, waiting on and sometimes running the bistro.

Her weekend job kept Hannah out of the cold, miserable house, but it was mainly to earn a bit of money and make it easier for her Mum financially as Hannah gave most of her pay to her. She had overheard her Mum asking John for a loan to pay the rent or they would be homeless and hoped that if she gave her money every week, it would help Abigail to pay off the debt. Her mum would be happier and they would still have a home.

Hannah got food into the bargain at the restaurant and made a good bit on tips too, but kept that nugget of information to herself as Abigail would want to borrow them and Hannah guessed she would never see the tips again.

In the end, Hannah ended up doing more "O" levels and got a couple of evening shifts to see if she could get her Mum out of the financial troubles that were getting serious. If Hannah worked more, she earned more and got a decent meal and Abigail was always grateful for any extra money on offer, saying it would help with one thing or another.

When Hannah had told Abigail of her plans, her mother had gone mad and begged Hannah to stay on for another year.

"We will be homeless and penniless in two months. Your Dad will stop paying and you *have* to do just one more year. I'll lose your family allowance too. One year, Hannah and I promise I will have a full-time job by then and we will be fine."

Hannah sighed and said that she would get the right qualifications to get into nursing but if she was not accepted by the NHS then she would be going into catering full time.

"At least I'll have food and warmth in catering and not have to put up with being half starved all the time. One year only, Mum, and that's it. I have to have a life and so do you, so I'll do this for both of us but you have to stick to your word."

Abigail smiled and went to hug her daughter but Hannah brushed past her with eyes bright from unshed tears and her lips white as she pressed them tightly together and stormed to her room.

****

Hannah was hardly ever at home and even when she was, Abigail was short tempered with her to the point that Hannah preferred to stay out of her way. When Hannah had suggested that her Mum went to the doctors for a pick-me-up, Abigail was furious.

"There's nothing wrong with me!" she screamed at her daughter. "I'm perfectly well and don't you ever say any different. Don't you think I've had enough of being told what to do and when to do it? Now get out of my sight and go and get your washing done. I'm not waiting on anyone hand and foot again so if you want clean clothes, you'd better learn how to use the washing machine and if you get your fingers caught in that mangle it's your own silly fault."

Hannah stared at her mother with complete surprise. Abigail had done the weekly wash yesterday and had dried and folded the clothes. They were waiting to be ironed and when Hannah had offered to do this task for her mother, Abigail had told her it was so kind of her to offer but it would give her something to do later.

Anyway, they had been using the twin tub for years and Hannah knew exactly what to do. There was an electric mangle that Hannah could remember being attached to a small washing machine that they had had in Thornton. Hannah smiled woefully as she recalled her mother cursing as her fingers got trapped then laughing when the smaller Hannah got upset begging her to be all right and feeling her mother's arms hugging her tightly and saying she was fine.

This sudden change in Abigail's behaviour was unsettling but Hannah knew better than to say any more and apologised before heading to the kitchen to get the iron and a few clothes she needed pressing for her waitressing job. Once the girl was organised, she ran upstairs to her bedroom. Better to iron on the floor in her room and be out of her mother's way rather than upset her further. Hannah decided she would ask Eileen to try and talk her mum into going to the doctor as something was not right and it was a worry. It was more than the money problems that were still not sorted out and Hannah was scared that her Mum was heading for a nervous breakdown.

Chapter 25.

"I never want to see you again, woman. Look at yourself! You are a damned disgrace and how do you think this looks on ME?"

Charles Hennessey was standing in his old house in Formby and the veins on his neck were standing out like deep red ropes as he was so angry.

"Evicted. The shame you have caused me is totally unforgivable and the sooner you are away from here the better. You are the talk of the town and people are saying it's MY fault. Well, it's not. You have had more money than needed to keep this place running but, oh no, Mrs Bloody Imbecile here needed more. Oh, and to say that you are glad to be going to somewhere as disgusting as Seaforth just shows how much time, energy and patience I have wasted on trying to turn you into something more than a common working-class fool with no desire to be better than anyone else. Well, get on with it, you disgusting, lazy bitch. I hope you enjoy yourself being back where you belong with the other people of this world who are nothing."

Abigail sat perfectly still next to the electric fire and refused to look at her ex-husband. It didn't matter anymore. He couldn't hurt her any more than she was already hurting and his words meant nothing. It was what she thought of herself anyway, well, most of it. When Charles realised his words were not having the desired effect, he announced that he was going.

"'Bye, Charlie," was all Abigail said as she continued to stare at the orange glow from the one working bar on the electric fire.

Charles was wrong, Abigail told the fire. The people she had met when Eileen took her to view the flat at Willow House were really friendly and Abigail knew in time that she would be happy. It was a relief not to be judged on how she looked by those she had met in the high rise. They had accepted her and this had given her the courage to think about a life without her husband's influence keeping her down at heel. A heel had a lot to answer for Abigail thought and she began to laugh until the hysterical sound turned to sobs that shook her whole body.

Abigail eventually cried herself to a standstill and realised she was fed up with the pain and anguish that had, if truth be known, started the day she said her marriage vows on a cold Boxing Day morning in a church in Accrington.

Charles had admonished her gently when he noticed that the heel on her not too white sandal had been nailed into place as she had walked down the aisle as a married woman. It was the hollow sound of every other step that made Charles notice something wasn't right with her footwear and when he had to stop and free the hem of her wedding dress that was somehow caught on her sling-back sandal, that's when he saw it. A nail holding the heel on the sandal. They had only just got outside the church when he had told her he was disappointed that she couldn't dress properly, today of all days. He had nipped her arm as he had hugged her and whilst still smiling had told her that he expected more and that she had to change her ways from this very second.

****

They were at the reception in the working men's club that all his family frequented regularly and he had told his sister to go and get a pair of her sandals for his wife to wear as he was embarrassed as the clip clop sound continued until they took their seats on the top table.

His family had sniggered and told him it was too late now he had put that ring on her finger and he had a lot of changes to make with this one, when his sister drunkenly announced to the whole party that she had got the footwear and waved them around for all to see.

Charles had laughed and told them that his new wife was everything he wanted and that she would no doubt have a few things to learn as he was going places and added hastily, she was too. The new bride blushed furiously and laughed as the tears danced in her eyes. No-one in the party apart from Charles, realised how upset and scared Abigail felt and presumed it was due to nerves of a newlywed that she had began to laugh too loudly and for too long.

"That's right, just follow my lead and do as I say and we will have a marriage that is happy, my darling," he whispered in her ear nipping her back as he slid his hand towards her shoulder. "Now, squeeze your big feet into these sandals and we'll say no more about it, for now."

****

The children had gone to live their own lives and she knew they would never return to the home they shared as a family. Well, now they couldn't even if they wanted to and Abigail hoped that they would come and see her regularly in her new home. It had upset her when she had told John and Hannah she was moving and they had done nothing more than nod when she had asked them to help her pack up the house and put the furniture into the new flat. There was no discussion and they didn't ask why. They knew.

It had been a living hell for Abigail living in this large, three bedroomed, semi-detached property for so long and at least where she was going would be easier to manage and less expensive to run as it was a one bedroomed flat. It was the lift that was going to take some getting used to as she was on the tenth floor and she wasn't good in small spaces. It made her panic. She had a week to get out and if truth be known, couldn't wait to give the keys back.

Eileen had been to help her every day and had scrubbed and cleaned each room as it was emptied with her friend. Eileen felt heart sorry for Abigail but kept her feelings quiet as she knew it would do neither of them any good to get maudlin. What was done was done. Eileen hoped that in time, Abigail would pick herself up and get to a place in life where she was content. As much as she would miss her natters every day with her friend and Eileen's two sons would no longer be able to see Auntie Ab as much, deep down it was the best thing for Abigail. As she sorted through the airing cupboard that was on the landing, Eileen hurriedly wiped her tear stained face on the corner of a sheet as Abigail's heavy footstep made the stair creak.
Chapter 27.

The final box had been put in the back of John's car and Hannah sat waiting for her brother to drive away. Abigail was watching them out of the upstairs bedroom window that overlooked the main road as the car pulled away. Neither of her children looked at the house that had been their home for the last ten years and Abigail knew that they were as relieved as her to be starting a new life.

She hoped it would be kind to them and that they would be happy. Not that it would take too much for that to happen, as it had been tough on all of them. Charles Hennessey had a lot to answer for and she had added to the mayhem that was life in Liverpool Road for her children as she had no idea how to survive without him, the man that was once her entire life.

If she could do one thing from this point on, it was to leave the past behind and learn how to stand on her own two feet. It would take time but there were no other options available. Well, there was one but she couldn't take her own life if her life depended on it as she was too scared to leave the children, just in case they needed her one day. For what? They seemed to be managing perfectly well on their own but maybe one day…

One day at a time, no matter how long it took and as she closed the bedroom door and headed down the stairs for the final time, she felt a lightness that had not been felt for years.

"Let's go, Eileen, take me home."

Eileen smiled at her friend.

Abigail stared out of the windscreen, determined not to look back at the house. It was forwards from this moment on. Once they had left Formby, Abigail sighed.

"All will be well, in time, all will be well," and as she wiped a single tear that had escaped, grinned at Eileen. "Come on, love, let's go and unpack that kettle. I could murder a cup of tea."

Printed in Great Britain
by Amazon

48801336R00097